GRAPHIC RECORDING

—

Live Illustrations
for Meetings, Conferences
and Workshops

—

gestalten

Table of Contents
—

Chapter 1
—
What Is Graphic Recording?
—

At some point or other, everyone has sat through a meeting and thought to themselves that nothing productive will come from it: too much information is thrown around for very little outcome. The same can be said about conferences, talks, and essentially any other form of professional gathering. The exchange of information in these settings is of fundamental value to move forward—no matter the project or the industry—yet guaranteeing effectiveness is extremely difficult. Maintaining alertness and concentration, even for those with the best intentions, can be trying, and the greatest ideas can be overlooked or forgotten once the gathering is over and everyone has returned to their daily grind. Synthesizing information, drawing pertinent conclusions, and defining clear goals is a challenge. This is where graphic recording comes in.
—

What Is Graphic Recording?
—

Graphic recording is a visual performance that complements a meeting, talk, or conference by visually summarizing the information communicated during those events. A graphic recorder will come equipped with their preferred tools (usually consisting of some large surface, such as a board or piece of paper, and high-quality markers or dependable chalk), ready to absorb all of the information that will be exchanged during the event and visually transfer it onto their chosen surface throughout the duration of the gathering for all to see, in the form of an easily understandable sketch or map that includes relatable drawings and words. The graphic recorder does this with a view to actively help achieve an engaging thought process around the ideas that were expressed, leading to a much more productive outcome. In other words, beyond documenting the content of an event, graphic recording allows for deeper engagement with the material, which results in more constructive follow-ups. While the creative industries are thought to be pioneers in out-of-the-box thinking and the first to embrace new methods, powerhouse firms such as Deloitte and leading players in the field of conferences such as the TED talks and the Global Economic Summit are among those adopting graphic recording as part of their strategy to do better business.

How Is Graphic Recording A Solution?
—

In essence, graphic recording transforms tedious and often pointless professional meetings into useful exchanges of information where the people present feel involved and consequently become more invested, for both their personal benefit as well as that of their company.

Many businesses have realized that despite technology and endless possibilities of engagement, we do not communicate very effectively. There is a need for better collaboration. We struggle with information overload and there has been a shift in how much data we receive and digest at a time. In order to avoid overload and attention fatigue, certain unwritten rules in our daily interactions with information have emerged, including, for instance, that a video should be no longer than three minutes, or that every article should have a summary at the top (and sometimes an estimated reading time). In the context of professional gatherings, techniques like graphic recording are tools that can master the overload aspect to deliver the essence of information while still being entertaining and catching people's attention. It's easier to stay involved and engaged if there's a sense of play. If the audience is entertained, then they aren't bored, and if they aren't bored, then they're more likely to take something away from the experience afterwards. Doodling is a natural activity. Coloring books for adults are a big trend these days.

And hand-drawn videos have become wildly popular online in the last couple of years. Using pen and paper focuses attention, relaxes, and stimulates the processing of information in a way that people can remember better.

Furthermore, the bulk of information we consume is arranged in a linear fashion—but that's not how we always think. Sometimes you need to jump back to an older idea. Sometimes you need to keep a few parallel ideas in mind at once. Graphic recording offers a chance to break out of the rigid confines of linear thinking. In business, presentations are mostly done in a linear format as well. PowerPoint slides are the classic example: one idea or chunk of information after another. If you miss something, it's gone. You can't go back, and it's difficult to create connections. In a graphic recording, the information is there all at once, and the viewer experiences it spatially. And bear in mind, non-linear doesn't mean the total absence of structure—it just means that the structure

follows a different logic. You make sense of things by looking at the big picture and relationships first.

Graphic recording also picks up on some of the features of storytelling and builds on them. It translates facts and figures into characters, emotions, metaphors, and dialogues. The pictures and graphical elements encourage users to create stories that viewers can participate in instead of bullet point lists that they scan and forget. As Jennifer Aaker writes in *Harnessing the Power of Stories,* "When most people advocate for an idea we think of a compelling argument, a fact or a figure. But research shows that our brains are not hardwired to understand logic or retain facts for very long. Our brains are wired to understand and retain stories." While the graphic recording isn't a story in itself, it can retroactively help communicate what was said during a meeting, conference, or brainstorming session in the form of a story, helping to share and interpret experiences.

Where Does Graphic Recording Come From and Why Is It Relevant Now?
–

Graphic recording is the natural outgrowth of historical precedents. You can trace information visualization back to hieroglyphs and cave drawings, which some argue were a very early form of graphic recording. Graphic recording is only a couple of decades old, and it came into being by emerging from other visual techniques. Similar techniques, like sketching or doodling, have been around for much longer. Graphic recording is an innovation in the sense that it combines those tools with new settings like meeting rooms and conference halls. It has a diverse set of roots across the business, design, and art worlds. There's a little bit of meeting culture and organizational development in its DNA (designing participatory processes, collaborative solutions, creating new forms of dialogue, and visualizing knowledge, for example). But elements of the pictographic work, graphic systems, and information design of people like Otto Neurath, Otl Aicher, and Edward Tufte are also present in its inspirations, and you can evidently see the influence of comics and storyboarding in it as well.

Graphic recording is embedded in the trend of visual thinking, which encompasses multiple disciplines like mind-mapping, video-scribing, sketching, and visual note-taking, to name just a few. Those techniques stem from our visual culture of design, illustration, and art. They have expanded into the disciplines of information design and are now progressing into today's text- and fact-oriented business world. What makes graphic recording stand out from many other visual techniques is that it is versatile—it can be applied to an infinite amount of topics, ranging from politics to medicine, from tech talks to educational content. It opens up new modes of perception and involves an artistic touch that makes information appealing, not boring. Each graphic recording can be viewed as a unique piece of informative art that invites you to look, explore, read, and wonder—and that hopefully encourages you to pick up your own marker and give shape to your own thoughts.

It makes sense that graphic recording is seeing a steady rise in demand and exposure at a time when visual storytelling and infographics are enormously widespread. Dan Roam, an expert in the field of visual thinking, notes in an article for the International Forum of Visual Practitioners that "pictures are a very, very powerful way to help us clarify the complexity [of ideas] and accelerate our understanding [of them] because our visual mind is so rapid and so able to visually parse complexity and find the patterns within it. Those things are very hard to do with words. It is hard to look at a complex idea expressed verbally and really see what it means. It is very difficult to take it apart, but if we can see it in a picture, it is very easy." Research and publications on multiple intelligences have given more momentum to the power of visuals (although the theory of learning styles is still debated). Visual thinking is common in approximately 60%–65% of the general population. Child development theorist Linda Kreger Silverman suggests that less than 30% of the population strongly uses visual/spatial thinking, while

another 45% uses both visual/spatial thinking and thinking in the form of words, and 25% thinks exclusively in words. The big takeaway from all this, as concerns graphic recording and people interested in making sure that listeners and participants really get the most out of a meeting, presentation, or workshop, is this: most people tend to remember auditory information better when it is supported by visual elements. And that is just what graphic recording does— it very effectively supports the key auditory information with visual elements, live and on-site.

How Does Graphic Recording Work?
—

Graphic recording's main stages are conferences and meetings (this book will mostly focus on graphic recording in these two scenarios), but it can adapt to different formats and has been used in a variety of settings. The most common form of graphic recording is usually done on big sheets of paper or foam boards. Graphic recordings can be performed by a single person or by a team of scribes. With teams working together, a graphic recording can sometimes merge into other formats such as knowledge walls, which

are visual boards where strategic reminders, trackings of lessons learned, or important information is shared for all employees to see, and to which they can contribute. Often documenting events over several days, these works can result in huge murals, impressive not only in size but also in content captured and through the world of pictures created.

On a smaller scale, but just as powerfully, graphic recordings can be used in meetings and group processes. For instance, scribes are invited into companies to draw change processes and organizational development. They visualize ideation sessions as well as small executive board meetings. If a team has a problem or wants to do some strategic planning and visioning, hiring a graphic recorder can help get them there faster. Of course, graphic recording can also happen outside the corporate world, in community or project work for example.

These types of graphic recordings are usually smaller scale (and produced in smaller rooms). The difference lies mainly in the fact these meetings are facilitated, dynamic processes rather than an agenda-based event like a conference. In settings like these, the nature of a graphic recording will often change and become less of a documentation technique and more a process tool. This is where graphic recording meets the

world of facilitation—and is mostly called graphic facilitation. While a graphic recorder will first and foremost be recording the event in real time and only sometimes choose to invite the audience to interact with the recording, a graphic facilitator will actively assist a group reach its goals through interactive methods. Graphic recorders can team up with facilitators to co-host a meeting or the illustrator can take the active role in steering the meeting and do a solo graphic facilitation. The attention is then split between working with the group and putting pictures on display. A graphic facilitator might also draw on other visual tools such as templates, dot voting, color coding with sticky notes, or collaborative drawing.

London-based visual company Scriberia sorts out the terminology like this: "The aim of graphic facilitation is to use images to prompt productive conversations, offer fresh perspectives, and pick new pathways through problems. It's a technique that, when done well, can change the way groups think, communicate, and collaborate." The bottom line is that graphic facilitation can help you move from a "nice to look at" visual documentation to creating a shared artifact of the team's work and experiences.

The particular benefit of graphic recording in any individual case depends on the setting and how it is used. Ideally, the graphic recorder is involved early on in the planning process of the event, enabling them to talk about the desired outcome and giving them time to brainstorm lots of possibilities to settle on the best choices for applying the visuals. There are essentially three different ways a graphic recorder can set up the performance, but in all cases it should be made clear from the start: either the audience can see the graphic recording only at the very end of the talk, or they can look at it during the process though only in a passive way, or finally they can be invited to interact with the graphic recorder while they are working on it.

Let's take a classic conference setting as an example. For lots of people who come from a visually more conservative culture, graphic recording is an exciting experience. It reminds them that thinking in pictures is natural for all of us and drawings have a power to capture our attention in a unique and appealing way. Still, they often initially praise the end product. Some time later in the experience, most people discover the depth of the technique as a thinking process. Turning praise into engagement and

getting people beyond the "pretty picture" state of mind is important if real value is to be drawn from visuals. There are a few ways to accomplish this: the facilitator can interview the graphic recorder on stage, or refer to and reflect on the visual, or ask the participants to point out what they find interesting. Whatever the approach, building in opportunities for people to interact with the information to process it in a meaningful way, especially if they're new to the technique, is of prime importance.

There is a common fear that graphic recording is a distraction from presentations, conversations, or other centerstage activities—but this is rarely the case. The graphic recorder and speaker should work together and complement one another, not be rivals, and the graphic recording should be viewed as a source of information and inspiration for the audience, available for taking their thinking to the next level. Indeed, a graphic recording becomes most effective when the group can see how their conversations are taking shape, so it is important to let people see the drawing as it grows, to brief the audience so they know what's happening, and to encourage them to take a closer look during breaks.

Main Benefits of Graphic Recording
—

More and more companies across all different sectors are hiring graphic recorders. Here's why.
—

Collaboration and Engagement
—

Graphic recording encourages collaboration, participation, and an inclusive process—both on an individual and group level. This results in stronger, more informed actions and decision-making. Graphic recording honors people's contributions and shows them they've been heard. The technique can be especially powerful for teams.

In his book *Visual Teams: Graphic Tools for Commitment, Innovation, and High Performance*, author David Sibbet coined the term "visual teams" and explains that those groups "use visual tools and methods to help them reach high performance in today's work environment. As teams become more and more global and distributed, visualization provides an important channel of communication—one that opens up the group's mind to improving work systems and processes by understanding relationships, interconnections, and big picture contexts."

Creativity and Reflection
—

Seeing spoken words be drawn acts as a catalyst—it boosts thought connectivity and the exchange of ideas, and stimulates imagination as well as creativity to open up different modes of perception. The full value of a graphic recording is tapped into when graphic recording is used as a tool for reflection. It allows participants to reflect on their thinking: "Are we seeing the same thing? Or do we perceive this differently?" It can inspire insights and mental connections. Graphic recordings take in not only the content of what is actually spoken, but also the emotion with which it is delivered. And graphic recordings do not just help us remember topics, they also help us think about them in productive ways.

Entertainment and a Fuller Experience
—

Graphic recorders are invited to capture content, but at the same time they are also there to perform. It is powerful to see someone capture ideas as they are occurring in real time, and people simply enjoy watching someone perform—graphic recording can make meetings or conferences more fun, which should not be underestimated. It is a way to enrich and deepen the group experience by going beyond business-as-usual and thinking outside the box, provoking people into more participation and a deeper thought process.

Enhancing Productivity
—

Graphic recording can help tackle information overload and enhance productivity. Our brain has limits. The conscious mind can pay attention to three, maybe four, things at once. By putting all the relevant information out there for all to see, graphic recording frees up our minds to concentrate on key details rather than trying to remember or write down everything that has been said. It reduces the cognitive workload, freeing mental resources for information-processing abilities.

Big Picture
—

Graphic recording distills ideas to their essence and increases clarity. It organizes ideas by drawing connections and relationships, enabling participants to see links between ideas and understand the bigger picture. All content is visible and can be referred to at all times, while slides and talks are fleeting and quickly fade from memory. This feature is especially valuable for events lasting several days, where graphic recording can act as a kind of external memory.

Mnemonics
—

Graphic recording appeals to visual learners. And since visual thinking is common in approximately 60%–65% of the general population, that means that you're reaching a significant majority of your audience. Graphic recording can also help increase the overall retention of information through dual coding (using words and pictures instead of just words to convey relevant information) and visual anchors (meaning that when you look at the graphic recording weeks later, memories are triggered by key words or images that summon the connected thoughts). That is also why a graphic recording can be interpreted differently by different people. It is not a detailed protocol, but rather a tool to trigger and associate the memories that a person has.

Documentation
—

Graphic recording is a logical complement or alternative to photo, video, or written documentation. It captures the content so it can be used, shared, and distributed later while helping everyone in the room connect, express, and contribute in new ways. The resulting documentation is clear and engaging. It summarizes and synthesizes the essence of conversations as they happen. It is available immediately and ready to share quickly after the event.

Sharing
—

An incredibly useful aspect of graphic recording is that it can be shared with people who were not present at the event to give them an insightful overview of what was said. It can act as the basis for further conversations around the topics that were discussed, and it enables a cascade of information and knowledge both during and after the recording.

recording. It takes the form of personal notes, though not for the entire audience to see, and can be incomplete or very subjective, whereas graphic recording aims toward a more objective way of documentation. It also lacks an aspect of interaction between the group and speaker, but just as with graphic recording, it is often used for conference documentation, is a great way to listen actively, enhances memory recall, and can easily be shared on the web. Sketchnoting is also very popular for school and university lectures, planning the next vacation, or even just drawing a shopping list.

Doodling encompasses quite a few other techniques like urban sketching, infodoodling, and product sketching. They are simple drawings that can have concrete representational meaning or may just be abstract shapes. They are usually not done with the intention of documenting or facilitating, but rather to create clarity of mind. Doodling can aid a person's memory by expending just enough energy to keep one from daydreaming. Sketching and doodling are more about the process and insights that might be gained during the act itself, and less about the end results. Doodling is usually done on a small scale, sketchpads, whiteboards, etc. It can also be a way to prototype and find new insights or a way to reach an agreement and common ground. Video-scribing refers to visual thinking techniques like drawing, illustration, or sketchnoting done in moving image. The most common technique is whiteboard animation. The term originally referred to the process of someone drawing on a whiteboard and recording it. The actual effect is a time-lapse, or sometimes stop-motion. With the introduction of software to create the whiteboard animations, the process has many different manifestations of varying quality. The most popular examples are hand-drawn whiteboard animations by Cognitive Media, who helped the RSA Animate series become a big success online with millions of views on YouTube. Video-scribe videos often remind people of watching a graphic recording for the first time. Although the techniques use a similar style and are both grounded in visual thinking and sketching, the process of making them is fundamentally different. While graphic recording is done live, a scribed video is usually a much longer process, consisting of scripting, voice-over, storyboarding, production, and post-production.

What Are Some Other Analog Techniques To Consider?

—

We stare at screens all day at work and then we go home and stare at them some more. It can be exhausting and isolating—the experience of seeing something that isn't on a screen is like a breath of fresh air, a surprise, and a welcome break. That in itself makes graphic recording a powerful way to engage an audience. In the past ten years the screen has become a ubiquitous device. We communicate via screens, we consume information and work on screens, do our shopping on screen devices. The screen has become the most important interface. But that ubiquity also creates a source of power for graphic recording, as there are substantial benefits to doing things offline

and offscreen. The Internet encourages skimming and browsing, while paper focuses and graps attention. There's just one thing to devote your attention to. Paper encourages deeper reading where the reader engages more thoroughly with the content than in its digital form. In a word, where presentations and meetings are mostly delivered using digital tools, graphic recording is the welcome analog counterpart.

As mentioned above, a general need for content to be visualized instead of just spoken and the rise of design tools in business are in part behind graphic recording's momentum. At the intersection of those disciplines and trends, a few techniques have evolved that support similar purposes, such as sketchnoting (also known as visual meeting notes), doodling, and video-scribing. Sketchnoting is like graphic recording's little sibling and has become a highly popular way to take notes in the past years. Very similar in its technique to graphic recording, it is a method to document meetings and conferences using graphics and words, but on a much smaller scale than graphic

Conclusion
—

Graphic recording has seen a steady rise in demand and exposure, but is still very new—which is incredibly exciting. This is a time when more and more companies in all kinds of different industries are understanding the need for new methods of collaborative thinking to reach higher levels of productivity, innovation, and creativity. Techniques such as graphic recording encourage thinking outside the box and respond to our non-linear way of processing information, and also stimulate discussions by personally involving participants, who become more invested as a result. While graphic recording's benefits are not yet quantifiable, they quickly become evident in qualitative ways: for instance, teams work better together when they have a graphic recording as a common reference point, participants are more likely to speak up when they know that what they are sharing will be taken into account by the graphic recorder, and people's mind power is better used when a graphic recording is being performed, as it allows them to spend their energy on generating ideas rather than keeping up with slides or taking notes. Its concept may be deceivingly simple, but that is exactly where graphic recording's groundbreaking quality lies—it hearkens back to certain analog basics while propelling you to future heights.

Chapter 2
—
How It's Done:
A Guide to Graphic
Recording
—

This section of the book will teach you how to
get your hands dirty and produce graphic recordings of your own. It explains how to prepare for
a graphic recording performance: how to think
about the content, what a client brief is and why
you need one, whether and how to use the speaker's own presentation (if one is available), and
how to do research before the big day. It gives
an overview of the tools of the trade: what you'll
need, how to get it to where it's needed, and how
to set it all up. Once you've mastered that, it will
be time to perform: that means listening, synthesizing, imagining, drawing (of course!), and
bringing it all together. Along the way you'll
face—and overcome—certain challenges. But
don't worry; this section also includes tips
on how to handle space and time, how to multitask, and more. And when you're all done, you'll
be able to add finishing touches, do a bit of
post-production—and maybe even go digital.
—

Chapter 2.1
—
How to Prepare
—

Preparing for a graphic recording can be both a very intense and very easy job. Just like any other creative process, there is no recipe for how to prepare perfectly. Each artist has their own workflow that suits them well. If you're an experienced scribe, preparation will most likely feel routine. If you're new to the job or thinking about doing a graphic re-cording, the right preparation might help you be less nervous about being on stage. No matter which segment you belong to, there are a few basics that are worth considering while get-ting ready to draw live: content, the client brief, the speaker's presenta-tion, research, and the event format.
—

Familiarize Yourself with the Content
—

Let's start with the content. To most people, graphic recording seems like a job done "on the spot" because all the drawings are created in real time and on location. This is true for the most part. No matter what, you'll need to think on your feet and quickly translate words into pictures, colors, and structures, right then and there. However, diving into the content before-hand can help you understand the bigger picture better and enable you to more easily generate images relevant to the topic. Especially if you know little about the subject of the talk, spend-ing some time getting to know what you will be drawing is a worthwhile investment. Here are a few ways to get savvy.

Review the Client Brief
—

Reading a client brief before the event can be really helpful—or confusing. Too much detail and your headspace gets clogged with informa-tion you might not need. After all, it is your job to summarize and bottom-line visually, not to produce a word-for-word protocol. Going through the agenda and getting a quick overview of the topic usually does the job. The goal of a good brief should be to get your image engine started, not to make you an expert in the field.

Sneak a Peek at the Speaker's Presentation
—

Sometimes it is possible to have a look at the speaker's presentation beforehand. This is helpful if the topic is really new to you, very technical, or filled with abbreviations and words you've never heard before. Browsing through the presentation can give you a sense of what it is about as well as how the talk will be structured. Jot down the key points you think are important. Don't try to memorize anything, though. Speakers often deviate from their slides, skip parts while talking, or add content shortly before.

Do Some Research
—

Research is a good way to get yourself acquaint-ed with a topic from different perspectives. Use search engines, online encyclopedias, blogs, and websites to get inspired. The more graphic recordings you do, the easier it will be to figure out how much research is necessary. It is very common to be called upon to draw events cover-ing a wide range of topics.

And Don't Forget to Find Out about the Event Format
—

As a graphic recorder, you're not only exposed to a multitude of topics and speakers, but also

How to PREPARE

Client Brief
- GET A QUICK OVERVIEW
- HAVE A LOOK AT THE AGENDA, SPEAKERS AND THEMES

PRESENTATION
- FIND OUT ABOUT THE STRUCTURE OF THE TALK
- JOT DOWN KEY POINTS
- GET INSPIRATION FOR VISUALS + METAPHORS

RESEARCH
- USE A VARIETY OF SOURCES LIKE WEBSITES, SEARCH ENGINES AND ICON LIBRARIES
- BECOME GENERALIST, NOT AN EXPERT ON THE TOPIC

BUILD A

CHAOS
ART
OUTSIDE THE BOX
CREATIVITY
IDEAS
NEW STUFF
MARKERS
SPARKS

Visual Vocabulary

to a wide variety of event formats. You may find yourself drawing a keynote, a panel discussion, maybe even a fishbowl session or a world café. You might also be asked to record brainstorming sessions, strategy meetings, or conversations at dinner receptions. Getting to know these formats and knowing how to give them a visual shape is a big part of the job. You can read up on them online and talk with the client beforehand to get a better idea of what they would like you to focus on capturing.

The Tools of the Trade
—

Graphic recording is a craft. And every craftsperson has their favorite tools. The tools you use shape your work, and a well-equipped toolbox is the best place to start. The basics for a graphic

recorder are something to draw with (like markers or pastels) and something to draw on (like paper or a whiteboard). There are some other tools that you may find helpful later for digitizing and sharing your graphic recordings, but we'll discuss them at the end of this chapter. Here, our focus is on getting started with the universals.

Things to Draw With
—

While you might find ways to make your own mark with other implements (fingerpaints, sand, digital tools), the two most common and useful drawing implements are markers and pastels.

Markers
—

There are different sizes and tips available (e.g., chisel, round tip, and brush tip). They're all

Graphic recording is a craft. And every craftsperson has their favorite tools. The tools you use shape your work, and a well-equipped toolbox is the best place to start.

great for different reasons. Try several types to find out which ones you're most comfortable with and explore the different effects you can create. Graphic recorders usually have three or more sizes in their arsenal and choose the size of the marker according to the canvas size and their personal drawing style. If you are going to work on a big canvas, opt for big markers. It will make writing headlines and drawing large visuals easier. Add smaller tips to your marker collection for creating hierarchies and adding

fig. 1

fig. 1
The Tools of the Trade illustration depicts the essential supplies needed for most graphic recordings.
—

fig. 2
Tools used for Sita Magnuson's Accelerating Innovation: Telling the Brain Story to Inspire Action, featured on pages 158–161.
—

fig. 2

details. The color palette is another consideration—some scribes are happy working with just a few colors or even black and white. Others love using a wider range. Have a look at the section on colors to find out how to choose the right palette for your work.

The brand of marker does not necessarily matter, and they differ from country to country anyway. Neuland is an old standby, while Sharpies, Faber-Castells, and Copics also work well. Again, the best approach is to try out several of them and stick with those you like best.

GUIDELINES AND TIPS FOR PICKING MARKERS

- Refillable markers are helpful, as you are going to use a lot of ink.
- Make sure you have a stable surface for refilling. Ink might spill, so make sure that the surrounding area is well covered.
- Opt for non-alcohol-based markers if possible. After a long day of drawing, the smell starts to matter.
- Shop for a belt pouch that can carry your markers during a graphic recording. That way your hands are free for drawing but you still have lots of other markers to choose from.

Pastels
—

Pastels are great for wider areas of color, e.g., sky, grass, arrows, etc. They give a softer touch to the visuals. They can be a little messy to apply, though. It is a good idea to bring some plastic to cover the floor, especially if you will be drawing in locations where cleanliness is an issue.

Things to Draw On
—

Paper, foamcore boards, and whiteboards are the most common and easily accessible drawing surfaces, though they are by no means the only options, as you'll see. Digital tools also open up some new avenues for drawing (more on that at the end of this chapter).

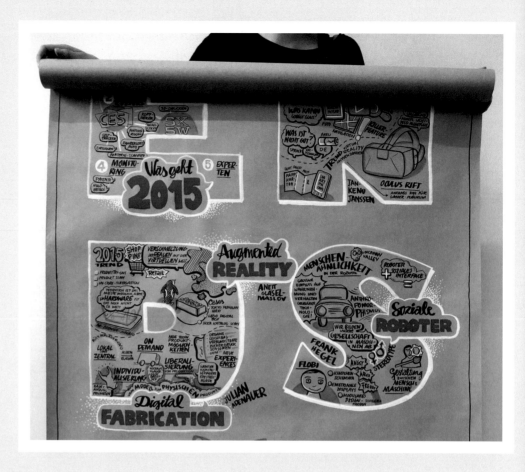

Paper
—

Paper is the most common material. It's easy to transport, it's cheap, the size can be adjusted, and if it's not too big, it can even be scanned for high-resolution reproduction. And it comes in all kinds of colors, which can create nice effects in combination with acrylic markers (a white marker on blue paper, for example). Make sure you handle it carefully, as it bends and folds easily. You should start with weights of 80 g/m² and up. The thicker the paper, the sturdier it will be, but the more ink it will soak up, so have your refill ready.

Foamcore Boards (KAPA)
—

A foamcore board covered with paper is essentially the same surface as paper, in terms of how you draw on it and what options are available, but it is more stable. Foamcore boards come in different sizes. They usually soak up less ink than paper alone. If there's no room to put up

some paper, a foamcore board represents an easy alternative—you can even put it on your lap to draw, if necessary.

Whiteboards
—

Whiteboards are a bit more difficult to draw on because of the smooth surface. You can't rest your hand on them, as you might wipe away what's already been written there. However, they also have the great advantage of letting you dry-erase any mistakes. On the negative side, the selection of colors and types of marker is smaller and the results will not last as long as paper or foamboard drawings. As a medium, it is much more "for the moment."

Other Materials
—

There really are no limits to what it is possible to draw on, especially if you are willing to experiment. You could try glass, chalkboards, light boxes, or even writing directly on the wall. Thinking further outside the box, there's also furniture, cars, houses, people—while you shouldn't pick an odd medium just for the sake of being different, never forget that you do have room to be creative.

When experimenting with new surfaces, pay special attention to how well the marker ink sticks to the surface. Sometimes you will need to opt for more permanent solutions like acrylic, lacquer, or paint markers.

GUIDELINES AND TIPS FOR PICKING SOMETHING TO DRAW ON

Paper is cheap, easy to carry, and an obvious first choice if you're starting out with graphic recording. Stop by your local art supply store to get your first fix.

- Bored with white paper? Change the backdrop and pick a new color. It makes for great contrasts with acrylic markers. Added bonus: you get to shop for new supplies.
- Feeling creative? Why not suggest drawing on a window in the meeting room or an office wall.
- Remember that graphic recordings can easily turn into large-size murals. Whatever you choose to draw on, go big!

Transporting and Setting Up Your Gear
—

Drawing on big surfaces also involves thinking about logistics. Some equipment like whiteboards or moveable walls will already be available at the location, but often enough you will have to arrange for something to be delivered.

How to Get Your Stuff There
—

Carry on: If you are only doing a short gig (like a one-day job), taking your materials with you should be easy enough. There are transport tubes for bringing paper along and markers will usually fit in whatever bag you're carrying. *Get it delivered:* Especially for foamboard, or if you're traveling a long distance to your job, delivery is advised. Ask your art supply store about their shipping conditions—they'll often be happy to take care of it for you.

How to Plan What Materials to Bring
—

Determining how much paper or foamboard to bring or how many markers to pack depends both on the way you draw as well as on the space available for your graphic recording. Talk to your client in advance to find out what the location looks like and how much space will be set aside, which will enable you to make a rough estimate. You can adjust your style to the space available, but always take more materials with you than you need. And be careful when traveling on planes—pressure changes may cause ink cartridges to leak, and security checkpoints may not permit liquids in your carry-on luggage.

Getting Set Up
—

A good setup for graphic recording makes the work much easier. As far in advance as possible, discuss with the client what's needed and how you'd like the drawing area to look. Talk about how much wall space there will be and what kind of materials you'll use.

You can go for moveable walls, flipcharts, easels, handmade setups, or even just draw on your lap if it's a small-scale graphic recording. The most important thing is that you have a solid surface to draw on that will not move much while you are working.

Ask for a small table where you can arrange your markers and tools as well as a chair. Graphic recording days are long and being able to take a break in between is most welcome. There should be some free space around your drawing area because you'll most likely be moving back and forth during the day. A graphic recorder's workplace is also a popular spot for participants to deposit their bags or charge their cell phones.

Make sure your drawing space is well lit. Especially at big conferences, rooms often have dimmed or colored lights, which will make it hard for you to choose the right colors and will also tire your eyes fairly quickly.

The most important thing to consider isn't visual, though: you need to be able to hear well. Make sure that you're either close to the person or the group speaking, or that you are positioned close to the loudspeakers. Nothing is worse that straining to hear all day long.

10 THINGS TO KEEP IN MIND WHEN PREPARING FOR A GRAPHIC RECORDING

1. Make a list of what to bring, and pack in advance.

2. Do some research if you feel unprepared.

3. Become a generalist on the topic you are drawing, not an expert.

4. Create a visual vocabulary around the topic.

5. Be well rested, calm, and relaxed.

6. Show up well in advance to get comfortable in your space and get everything ready.

7. In your mind, be over-prepared, yet under-structured.

8. Be comfortable with your tools.

9. Zone in on what's going on in the room—people, process, content.

10. It's all about visualizing what's in front of you, but it's not about you.

Chapter 2.2
—
How to Perform
—

Watching a graphic recorder work is mesmerizing. Starting with a blank canvas, the visual slowly unfolds over the course of the day. By the end of the event there's a huge piece of work on display. Participants often say that it's quite relaxing to watch that process. For a graphic recorder, however, it's intense. Graphic recording is multitasking writ large.

In a nutshell, scribing is a four-step process. While paying attention and listening to what's been said, the graphic recorder needs to synthesize, bottom-line, and distill meaning from conversations. This is the "silent" part of graphic recording—you don't see it, but it is essential preparation for the resulting work. After all the information has been processed, pen is put to paper and it's time to draw.

Broken up into pieces, it is a fairly straightforward process. What makes graphic recording both very appealing and very difficult is that it is done in a continuous loop. There are no breaks in between a talk, no time for thinking thoroughly about what or how to draw, and no possibility to rewind and listen to something again.

In the world of music, there is a term called "circular breathing." It is a technique used by players of some wind instruments, like the saxophone or flute, to produce a continuous tone without interruption. What those musicians do is breathe in through the nose while simultaneously pushing air out through the mouth using air stored in the cheeks. A graphic recorder's technique is similar. We breathe in conversations, store key messages, translate them into pictures, and produce visuals simultaneously, without interruption.

Like all artistry, it takes practice to perform all that at once. But by looking at the single steps, graphic recording reveals itself as a craft that can be mastered bit by bit: listening, synthesizing, imagining, drawing, and bringing it all together.
—

Step 1: Listening
—

Are you a good listener? What makes a good listener? How do you listen? And what do you listen to? Listening well is a condition for doing graphic recording. What you hear is what you'll draw, and what you don't will never make it into your visual.

Listening is an activity. Unlike listening to your radio as background noise, you are on high alert when listening for a graphic recording. The purpose is to gain information from the speaker, construct meaning from those verbal messages, and create anchors for others who will later use your visuals to recap the content.

However, that does not mean that you have to catch every single word. Rather than making a transcript of what you're hearing, the focus is on bottom-lining. That means that roughly 10% or less of what's being said actually makes it onto the canvas. The goal usually never is to capture ALL content, but to form a coherent picture.

In graphic recording, you listen with intention. There are many approaches to what to listen for. We'll take a look at some examples. First, though, we should cover some guidelines and tips for listening.

GUIDELINES AND TIPS FOR LISTENING

- Find a spot in the room where you can hear well.
- Anticipate making notes (on Post-its or a piece of paper).

As the person is speaking:
- Focus completely on what they are saying.
- Mentally note the main points they are making, ready for summarizing.
- Don't think about your own ideas. This will prevent you from getting distracted or forgetting what the person has said.
- Listening usually requires more energy than speaking, as it involves receiving and interpreting the information.

With those points in mind, we can move on to specific approaches to listening. As noted, there are several ways to go about it, but the following three are perhaps the most relevant for graphic recording: informational listening, pictorial listening, and emotional listening.

Informational Listening
—

The process of informational listening focuses on the ability of an individual to understand a speaker's message. To help zero in on the speaker's message, you can take cues from the purpose and structure of the talk, key words, and quotes.

Purpose: The purpose of the talk can help define listening patterns. Is it a talk about the future? Then listen for scenarios and visions. Is it a meeting about next steps? Then listen for calls to action and concrete advice.

Structure: "My talk today is about three things"—this is how a lot of presentations begin. It is also a great hint about how to listen or what to listen for. Presenters often clue the audience in on how their talk is structured to give them a better overview. Use that to your advantage.

Key words: Key words are easy to catch. They are often repeated and usually nouns (like "innovation" or "sustainability") or strong verbs (like "move forward," "align," or "cooperate"). Try to keep count—if you hear something more than three times, it most likely plays an important role in the speaker's message.

Quotes: Taking a line from a talk or picking up a quote from a comment is a charming way to breathe some life into your content. It also helps establish a direct connection with your audience. When people discover that what they have said is drawn or written in the graphic recording, it is not only a pleasant surprise, but highly appreciated as well.

Pictorial Listening
—

Pictorial listening means listening for metaphors and comparisons that are ripe for graphic treatment, like "the coming months will be turbulent—the whole crew will help out on deck and strong leadership is needed to guide us through the storm." Metaphors are often used for storytelling or when adopting a more emotional approach to capture the audience.

Emotional Listening
—

Emotional listening is a matter of focusing on humor and atmosphere. Did you hear the audience laugh? Gasp? Be surprised? Paying attention to those moments and drawing them can be a nice way to take your visualization beyond mere content. Listen not only to the words that are said, but also to the speaker's tone of voice and body language.

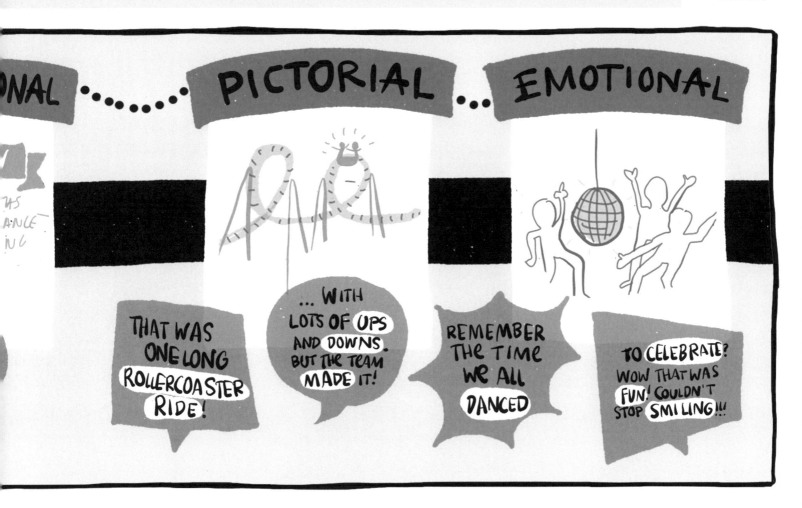

fig. 1

fig. 1
The 3 Ways of Listening
illustration depicts the
three strategies used by
graphic recorders when
working on a job.
—

fig. 2
Ink Factory drawing live
for the Urban Innovation
event featured on pages
130 and 131.
—

fig. 2

Step 2: Synthesizing
—

Synthesizing is two things—filtering and pattern building. Filtering means throwing away 90% of what you hear and keeping 10%. The actual ratio will vary depending on the focus of your graphic recording, but in any event, you will only be using a fraction of what you hear.

As for pattern building, while you are listening, key messages are stored in your memory. During synthesizing, those messages are formed and connected. That's pattern building. The patterns can be based on a number of factors, like similarity (key messages and evolving clusters). Pattern building requires a long attention span and the ability to retain a lot of information at once. Memory is essential to the listening process because the information we retain when involved in the listening process is how we create meaning from words. We depend on our memory to fill in the blanks when we're listening. Because everyone has different memories, the speaker and the listener may attach different meanings to the same statement. When multiple graphic recorders draw the same talk, the outcomes are often vastly different. Synthesizing will help you put all the pieces together and reduce complexity.

GUIDELINES AND TIPS FOR SYNTHESIZING

- Continuously summarize the main points that have been made and don't take too long to bottom-line.
- Even if you disagree with the speaker's point of view, summarize what they have said first.
- You don't have to represent everything they say—just the key points.
- Go beyond mere summaries and try to find overarching themes. Graphic recording is non-linear, which lets you connect content from different parts of a talk.

Step 3: Imagining
—

Graphic recording means using ALL of your brain. Listening and synthesizing are focused on language and logic, while imagining and drawing involve handling spatial information and visual comprehension. The left brain/right brain dichotomy is a myth, though: today, neuroscientists know that the two halves of the brain collaborate to perform a broad variety of tasks and that the two hemispheres communicate through the corpus callosum.

Looking at a presenter's charts can definitely help and inspire, but is not necessary for a graphic recorder. That is because imagining is about creating a visual image in your mind's eye. That image is what you'll use to translate what you hear and synthesize it into a graphic representation. Imagining happens on small scales (like translating a single word into a picture) but also on medium and large scales (like creating visual hierarchies, or estimating the space you have left on your paper and drawing accordingly, etc.) During the imagining phase, you rely heavily on your visual vocabulary. Some images are created spontaneously, but most will be drawn from the repository of images stored in your memory. There are multiple design elements, ranging from pictorial elements such as symbols and icons to elaborate drawings of outlines, landscapes, and characters (see separate chapter on design elements). The bigger your visual vocabulary, the faster you can process information and translate it into images. Musicians do something similar when they improvise. They know the key and the scale, which gives them a supply of appropriate notes (their repository), and that enables them to create music on the spot without knowing what they'll be playing in advance.

GUIDELINES AND TIPS FOR IMAGINING

- Research the topic you'll be drawing. This can help expand your visual vocabulary.
- Use a visual search engine like Google Image Search to find inspiration.
- Your mind's eye is like a muscle: give it a workout by writing a list of complex words and thinking about what they look like without drawing them.

fig. 1

Step 4: Drawing

—

You're going to have to draw if you want to be a graphic recorder. But the good news is, there's no one right way to draw. If it works for you and it works for your clients, that's all that matters.

You can't train to be a graphic recorder (yet), so graphic recorders come from a wide variety of backgrounds: self-taught, trained illustrators, architects, storyboarders, comic artists, business consultants, moviemakers, photographers, graphic designers, scientists, etc. All those different influences result in many styles.

Graphic recording takes place in real time, so it is important to find a style that you can use in real time, too. Keeping things simple is often the key. Remember, most of the work is done live, sometimes mixed with elements that

are pre-drawn (like headlines, visual containers, portraits, etc.) or added afterwards (like shading, color, connecting arrows, content sketched on a note during the talk, etc.). Think stick figures, not elaborate portraits, and don't feel pressured to produce works of art.

The resulting visuals may look chaotic, like a *Where's Waldo* illustration, or they may seem like very structured infographics. That's OK: the style of a talk can heavily influence your drawing. Speakers who read out bullet point lists will trigger different images than storytellers will. A group discussion will look different than a well-structured keynote. In any case, graphic recordings are composed of more than just pictures. They will also incorporate text, colors, structure, and flow (more on this in the chapter on design elements). Every graphic recorder has a different element ratio. Some predominantly use typography, others draw mostly pictures. Graphic recordings can range from black-and-white sketches to colorful murals.

GUIDELINES AND TIPS FOR DRAWING

• Keep it simple.
• Find your own style.
• Start your own visual vocabulary.
• Look at other scribes' work for inspiration until you develop your own visual style.

> You're going to have to draw if you want to be a graphic recorder. But the good news is, there's no one right way to draw. If it works for you and it works for your clients, that's all that matters.

fig. 2

fig. 1-3
Sita Magnuson's step-
by-step preparation
process for Accelerating
Innovation: Telling the
Brain Story to Inspire
Action, featured on pages
158–161.

fig. 3

Step 5: Bringing It All Together
—

A graphic recording may be a loose collection of symbols, characters, and words that looks more like wild scribbles than an informative document, and yet the mind is able to recognize certain patterns by itself. But just because the audience is capable of making sense of a jumble of images doesn't mean that there are not ways that a graphic recorder can enhance readability and understanding by combining design elements in certain ways. Specifically, you can work to create hierarchy, flow, coherence, and depth.

Creating Hierarchy
—

Hierarchy is about working in levels. Text and images usually have different sizes. You can intentionally split them into levels to create a clear and easy-to-read hierarchy. Depending on the size of the drawing, this might be just two levels or as many as five or six. There are several ways to visually create hierarchy: varying text size, adding color, and emphasizing certain elements with banners, shading, etc. For headlines, consider uppercase letters that stand out from the rest. Use smaller text for items within "lower" categories, like headlines for smaller agenda points or sub-headlines. Make sure to stick to the same size when items are on the same level. When working with color, use dark colors for text and outlines and lighter ones for shading and highlights. If you want to make it clear that certain elements are more important than others, you can also use shading or dimensionality to make them stand out. If it's a word or phrase that needs to be emphasized, consider turning it into a banner or putting a box around it. Remember—since a graphic recording is a non-linear representation of the talk, you're not limited to typical top-to-bottom, biggest-to-smallest methods of showing hierarchy, and the various tools in your arsenal will enable you to find your own solutions as you go along.

Creating Flow
—

Part of your job as a scribe is to guide the viewer's eye with graphic elements. Rather than sketching a series of static drawings, you'll be creating attention, flow, and movement. Don't feel like you need to do all that as you go—it is also easy to insert afterwards. The primary means of creating flow is through picturing relations—that is, adding little details that indicate how parts of the visual relate to each other. For instance,

HOW TO CREATE FLOW

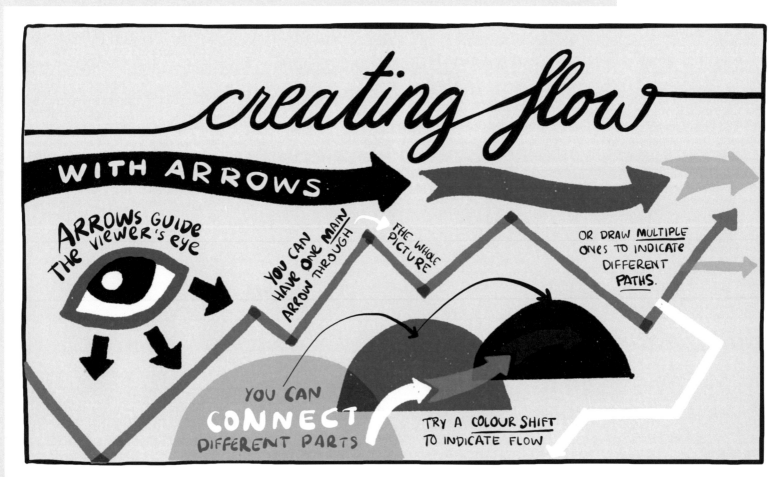

creating HIERARCHY

- IS ALL ABOUT WORKING IN LEVELS
- TEXT MIGHT HAVE DIFFERENT SIZES
- HEADLINES ARE **BIG**
- SUBHEADLINES LIKE THESE ARE SMALLER
- ADD FRAMES, BOXES OR BANNERS TO HIGHLIGHT CERTAIN PARTS
- WORKS FOR TEXT AS WELL AS IMAGES

DARK COLOURS FOR OUTLINES

LIGHTER COLOURS FOR SHADING

arrows depict order, effects, interdependence, or correlation. They can also indicate influential factors, options, results, and development. Lines and paths as well as physical connections between items are related techniques. And you don't need to limit yourself to literally drawing the flow—you can create it verbally using lists, for instance, or on a meta-level by using color. For example, the coloring could shift from blue to green to indicate progress through an idea or process. This is also an example of the kind of detail you can add or refine later. Perhaps you'll have begun with blue and ended with green—you'll be able to go back later and shade in different gradations to better visualize the flow.

Creating Coherence
—

Coherence is about repetition: repetition in color (color-coding), repetition in shapes and forms (similar characters, line weight), repetition in typography (size and style), repetition in structural elements (frames, boxes, etc.).

If creating flow is about picturing relations, creating coherence is about repetition. It's easier to read an image if you have visual anchors that reappear, especially on large images like graphic recordings. Think of it like a legend on a map—everything that's red can, for example, signal importance. Every sentence written in the same size and width will be indicating the same hierarchy.

We as humans have a simple way of making sense of the world: we group things that are similar, look alike, are close to each other or move in the same direction. It helps us break down complexity and understand visuals more quickly.

Creating Depth
—

Creating depth means adding dimensions and lifting items off the page. Graphic recordings may be made on flat canvases, but they do not have to look flat themselves. Shading is an easy and effective means of creating depth. You can do so by adding crosshatching, stippling, filling,

contours, drop shadows, cast shadows, etc. Layering or stacking elements on top of each other is another means of creating depth. Other design techniques that can create depth include patterns, negative space, backdrops, and effects like stretching words. Depth also refers to the general physicality of the drawing. For instance, cartoon details can create a sense of action and movement. Things like big drops of sweat that spring off the foreheads of anxious characters, clouds of dust that hang in the air in place of a swiftly departing character or object, speed lines that trail after quickly moving objects, wiggly lines around shaking objects, etc.

> Graphic recordings may be made on flat canvases, but they do not have to look flat themselves. Shading is an easy and effective means of creating depth.

The Big Four—Your Graphic Building Blocks
—

In attempting to bring everything together, you're going to need building blocks. You'll need to be able to answer graphic recording's own chicken-vs.-egg question: "What came first, the words or the pictures?" The question of how a visual begins will probably be answered differently by each artist for each event. Listening patterns usually determine what you pick up and how you transform it. Nevertheless, whenever you put the pen to the paper, you'll have to choose between text and something visual. "Visual" is itself a fairly broad category, so if we refine the term further, we arrive at the big four: the key building blocks of any graphic recording. They are: text, shapes, structure, and color. The elements can stand alone, but they can also be combined. A word might be stylized to the extent that it looks like a picture. A line that's simply a shape might give structure to the whole visual. Or text and image may combine to form a sequence like something from a comic strip. So the big four are not a way to categorize all the elements of a graphic recording, but rather an attempt to understand how it is composed and how the elements play together.

Structure
—

Each graphic recording has a different build-up, but there are patterns that can be summarized. In each graphic recording you can look for an overall structure as well as "micro- structures," smaller entities that also help the eye navigate the content. You can have a vague idea of how you would like to do an overall structure for the visual beforehand. It does not make sense to impose a detailed structure upon a graphic recording. Live situations are too volatile to rely on agendas, time, and promised content. You can brainstorm ideas in advance, but ultimately you will have to react to what the speaker actually says. In the end, how the content is delivered (time, speaker, style) will be the determining factor for the visual structure.

A graphic recording reflects the structure of the event. If you are recording a messy group discussion, the visual most likely will also be chaotic. While structural elements can help shape a conversation and make it look more linear/tidy than it actually was, it cannot make visual sense out of nonsense talk.

When talking about structure, we can break the concept down into the overall structure and microstructures. Overall or basic structures create a layout for a visual. They can range from an abstract graphic approach with lines and boxes to a more concrete, pictorial way to visualize things. Microstructures, on the other hand, refer to the structures you will create in between smaller items. They can be done ad hoc or even after the visual is done.

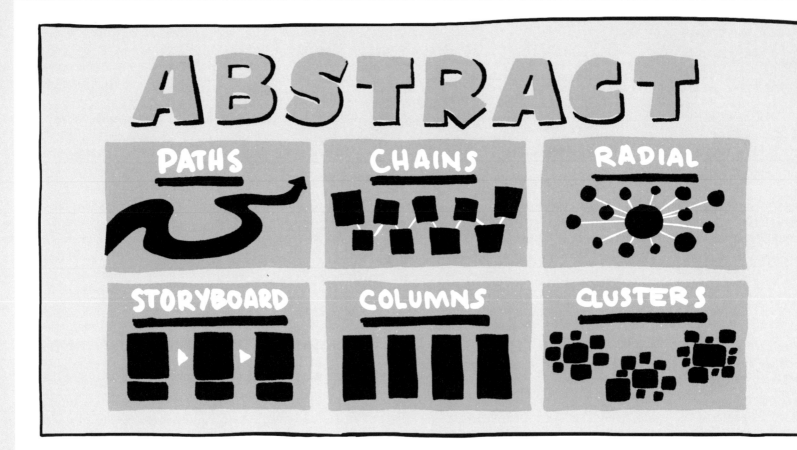

Examples of Basic Structures

Abstract:
- Path, lines: An ongoing line with a beginning, end, and stops in between. A line can start anywhere and go anywhere.
- Chains: A chain of containers (e.g., big arrows), working from left to right.
- Radial system: Content is arranged around a central focal point and radiates outwards. It can be done with circles, cycles, mindmaps, etc.
- Popcorn: The most versatile structure, as you can arrange content any way you'd like and connect it with lines and arrows. Can be clusters.
- Columns: From left to right, top to bottom.
- Storyboard: A sequence of panels that looks a bit like a comic strip.
- Grids: Horizontal and vertical boxes arranged in grids. Simple, geometric layout; looks very tidy.

Concrete:
- Landscapes: With horizons, mountains, paths, clouds, rivers, pathways, etc.
- Containers like key visuals (hot air balloons, cars, etc.)

Examples of Microstructures
- Arrows: They create focus, flow, a sense of direction, processes, paths, or relations between items.
- Separators: Elements like lines for distinguishing ideas, agenda points, talks, etc.
- Bullet points: For lists where content is delivered densely. Separate the list items and give each a bullet point.
- Frames and boxes: They group a set of ideas together and separate them from others. Remember: Draw or write the content first, then draw the enclosing lines so that you avoid having to squish things into too small a space.
- Speech bubbles: For containing content like ideas, and making them distinct.
- Connectors like lines (dotted lines for loose connections, thick lines will signal stronger links, thin for ones weak ties, etc.).

GUIDELINES AND TIPS FOR BUILDING A GOOD STRUCTURE
- Especially for large-scale drawings, bringing a pencil can be really helpful to trace large items before using a permanent marker. You can erase the sketch later.
- Leave enough white space. It is an important component that will allow you to add structural elements like boxes and arrows after you've jotted down text and images.
- You can see levels of organization from a distance. It helps to think in two or three levels to design graphic recordings. Imagine you're standing directly in front of one, then one meter away, and then ten meters away. You will see different levels of detail depending on where you stand, and should take that into account.

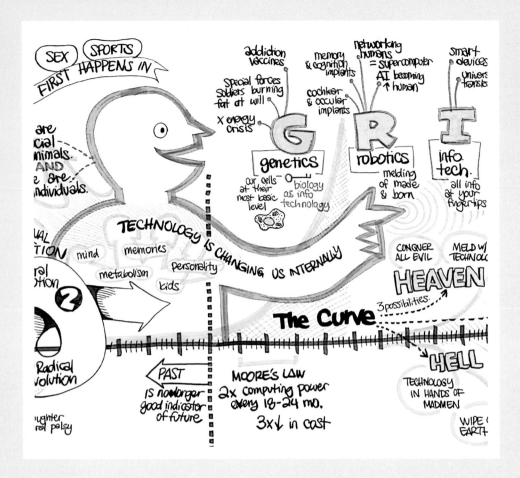

Just because the whole rainbow is available does not mean that you should use all of it. Limit your colors and create a color palette. It will help you create a better structure.

the best way to ensure that you're using color well is to get a bit of distance and see what your audience sees. Taking a step back from the visual will help determine if and where color is needed.

Words
—

Words make up a big part of a graphic recording. It's the combination of words and pictures that makes graphic recordings powerful. Words are often the first element added to a graphic recording. They require little to no translation, can be jotted down quickly, and are very precise (whereas visuals and metaphors require more interpretation). Words can refer to the more artistic use of lettering as typography, typefaces, and calligraphy, as well as content in written form like quotes, headlines, or specifics from the talk.

It is possible to create a graphic recording that consists mainly of words with hardly any pictures. Doing so can still result in a visually appealing image that can be read and understood. However, relying too much on words alone risks missing out on the positive mnemonic effects of dual coding. Whatever design elements you use, it is important to be consistent and create a unified style.

Some Hints for Working with Words

As all the words in a graphic recording are handwritten, it is important to put some effort into legibility. Aim for a good balance between writing fast and writing legibly (illegible words are no help to anyone).

If you make a mistake, there are three quick ways to correct it: writing over it (if possible), using correction fluid for minor corrections, and sticking mailing labels over larger areas.

Colors
—

You have a whole rainbow at your disposal for different purposes and effects. While black and white may seem more sober and official, you should feel free to spice things up. Color theory and a color wheel can serve as helpful guidelines when selecting colors, but in many cases, the colors you use are a matter of personal style. Color can also capture the atmosphere of a room, display the company's corporate colors, be realistic, or create an emotion.

There are several other reasons to use color:
- To support structure: e.g., the first chart is yellow, the second is blue, the third is green, etc.
- To create similarity: People often perceive similarly colored items as part of a group or pattern.
- To create opposition: When similarity occurs, an object can be emphasized if it is dissimilar to the others.
- To create highlights and emphasis.
- To create general attention.

Color can also be used as a background—you can experiment with black cardboard, blue backdrops, or tinted glass. Experimenting with colors is even easier when working digitally. Acrylic paints will come in handy if you are trying to draw and write on colored surfaces.

Some Additional Tips for Working with Colors

Just because the whole rainbow is available does not mean that you should use all of it. Limit your colors and create a color palette. It will help you create a better structure. Use color-coding to assign colors to certain parts of the visual. Remember the basics of warm/cold, complementary, and analogous colors and their effects on perception. Shades of a color (blue, light blue) are perceived to be very similar and all content using those colors will be grouped together. Analogous colors (blue, purple) will be perceived as similar. This works well for doing a gradient effect in a graphic recording. Complementary colors, on the other hand, work like opposites and imply conflict or differences. And finally,

Be especially careful when writing headlines. They are hard to correct due to their size.

Shapes
—

There are a variety of shapes (what most people would consider drawings) in graphic recordings. The most common are symbols and icons, illustrations and pictures, people and characters, and key visuals.

Symbols and icons are things most of us experience in everyday life—emojis on our smartphones, icons on our computers, symbols on the subway, etc. They are part of cultural conventions and are easy to decode. You can create them by reducing "real" things (mobile phones, vehicles, everyday objects) to simple shapes and forms. Since they are simplified, they are easy and quick to draw. Symbols are often used as a fast way to visualize and when there is no time for elaborate pictures or illustrations.

Illustrations and pictures are more elaborate drawings or combinations of several symbols, icons, and characters. They are used to describe more complex ideas that cannot be expressed with a single icon. It is often easier to create a visual message with a combination of elements than to attempt to pick just one perfect symbol or word.

People and characters range from stick figures to portraits to fully developed characters. While it takes a bit of skill and practice to properly draw people in a short time, you do not need to draw detailed characters to make the meaning clear. Simple is often best, and the way that you draw characters can become part of your signature style—it is a way to make your work distinctive and easily recognizable. Characters are often placed in comic strip–like panels with dialogue, which are great for telling stories. Symbols and icons also often merge or morph into characters—just add arms, legs, and eyes to bring an object to life. On a more reality-based note, including sketches of the speaker with quotes is a standard feature of many graphic recordings.

Key visuals often work as containers where the outline is the shape and all content is filled into that container. Working for a car manufacturer, an obvious key visual would be a car, a tire, or a road. They can also be more abstract, like a landscape or geometric shapes. Key visuals

often pick up on the theme of the event. They work especially well from a distance, because the viewer can focus on the overall impression rather than specific details. If you are performing before a large audience, key visuals will be an important part of your toolkit.

Combining Text and Shapes

Words and images are often combined to create a more explicit or deeper meaning. How do words and images go together?

- One-to-one: The image depicts the word and the word describes the image. This is often done when the word(s) already employ(s) a metaphor. For example, talking about "extending an olive branch" will easily translate into exactly that.
- Text transformed into visual metaphors: Sticking with the example of the olive branch, the image might also include a dove carrying the branch. Metaphors are often cultural conventions.
- Contradiction: Drawing the exact opposite of the word.
- Stand-alone: Pictures do not necessarily accompany words. They can also speak for themselves without additional detailed explanations.

- Word pictures: Words can act as pictures—think of the word "car" written so that it forms the shape of a car.
- Add-ons: Pictures can elevate parts of the text, add an emotional level to the words, or comment on them—and vice versa.

GUIDELINES AND TIPS FOR MANAGING YOUR BUILDING BLOCKS

- Start with what comes most naturally to you—text, shapes, structures or color. There is no right or wrong in graphic recording, just your personal style and a mix of the proper ingredients
- Find inspiration in other visual artists' work and add your personal touch to create your very own unique way of scribing. Not just graphic recorders, but also illustrators and designers, maybe even street artists and painters.
- Too much color or too much chaos for your liking in your pictures? Go for KISS—keep it short and simple. Focus on only a building block or two; it'll help to master them bit by bit.

How to Handle Challenges
—

Every discipline has its own challenges. To be successful as a graphic recorder, you will need to do more than just draw. You'll also need to be able to manage space and time, multitask, stay focused, and handle your audience, which may include non-visual people and even (shock!) critical voices.

How to Handle Space
—

"How do you make sure everything fits on your canvas when you don't know what the speaker is going to talk about?" That's one of the most frequently asked questions about how graphic recording is done. Luckily, there are several little tricks that you can use to plan how to use the available space.

First, find out how much space you have in total. Compare your space to the agenda and make a rough estimate of how much you'll use for a certain period of time. This really only works as an estimate, as schedules often change and content can be dense (packed with a lot of facts) or stretched (like storytelling, for example). If you're a beginner, drawing from left to right on an endless roll of paper can really help. Just cut the paper once you're done—no need for planning, and you'll always have room. Once you're more experienced, you can choose a starting point—left, middle, top, or bottom—and make your way through the visual. Many roads lead to Rome. You'll find your path while walking it.

The size of your writing and your individual drawings, as well as how much white space is in between, will have a huge influence on the overall size of your drawing. An experienced graphic recorder will be able to adjust the size according to the space available. If you find yourself running out of space, you can filter a bit more and record less content. Be sure that the overall ratio of space given to each topic or speaker is appropriately balanced (e.g., a one-hour talk should have a larger visual representation than a ten-minute slot).

If you discover gaps in your graphic recording and there is no more content to draw, you can fill them with other items like:

- Local landmarks (let's say the event is in Berlin: the TV Tower at Alexanderplatz would be a nice addition).
- The date and the name of your location.
- Scenery or a drawing of the location itself.
- Portraits of speakers.
- An additional key visual, symbols, or icons.
- Anecdotes or observations you made.
- Patterns, colors, or something artistic that you feel fits well.

How to Handle Time
—

Graphic recording is a live performance. You only have a limited amount of time to draw or to go back and touch things up, and there's a constant stream of information that you'll need to filter and synthesize at the same time. Time will always be a factor affecting your work, but there are ways to deal with it. You'll need to be ready to go as soon as the talk or the conference starts, so be sure to plan time to set up. Be there well before the event starts. This will give you the opportunity to get set up in a quiet, uncrowded room. You'll be able to mount your canvas, get your markers ready, and zone in on the topic of the day.

Once you're set up, the big factor is time during the talk itself. Start scribing as soon as the talking starts—there is usually very little extra time available to finish drawings later, so make the most of what you have. Draw in stages—if the speaker progresses too quickly, start with parts of a sentence or a drawing and finish it later on. If there's too much content delivered at once, make quick notes on a sticky note or on the canvas with a pencil and finish it afterwards. Keep this to a minimum because you'll have to use your breaks or stay longer after the event. If you miss something, ask the speaker to repeat it. If the setting is informal and you're interacting with the audience or the speaker, asking them to specify or repeat certain parts shouldn't be a problem.

Luckily, graphic recording isn't usually one big rush. During longer talks or conferences, there will be breaks that you'll be able to use for your own work. Use them to finish details that you didn't manage to complete while the talk was going on. Talk to people to get some feedback or input. Do some spell-checking. Step back and take a look at the layout and overall impression of your visual so that you can approach it better when the talk resumes.

And remember that your job doesn't end when the talking stops. Plan some time for finishing touches after all the talking is over. Depending on your experience, you might be able to finish up in just a few minutes, but you may need up to an hour or two.

Multitasking and Avoiding Blackouts
—

There's another question graphic recorders are frequently asked: "How do you do this all at once? And all day long?" When experiencing a graphic recording for the first time, many people see the product, the visual itself, first, but it soon dawns on them that drawing while listening and synthesizing is quite a cognitive achievement. It takes focus and stamina to multitask all day long, but it's definitely doable. Try shorter time spans when you get started and you'll notice that your endurance will increase the more you practice. When your mind is engaged on so many levels at once in the midst of a constant flow of information, blackouts are always a risk. You can minimize the risk of zoning out and missing key details by getting plenty of sleep before the event, getting into the flow, and staying hydrated, eating well (and regularly!), and avoiding too much sugar.

Handling the Audience
—

For a newcomer, the idea of performing in front of a large audience might seem intimidating. Don't let that stop you from giving it a try! While the graphic recording is typically visible to the audience while the talk is in progress, that does not have to be the case. Graphic recording can be done in solitude somewhere in the back of the room, or right there on stage with the speaker, or somewhere in-between. Your positioning will usually be agreed upon in advance. In many cases, the layout of the location will determine where you'll be drawing (after all, the job does have certain space requirements). But it is often possible to discuss your personal preferences with your client. While graphic recording is certainly not a job for misanthropes, there is good news if you are a bit shy: you can work with your back to the audience. Musicians are sometimes called "shoegazers" when, instead of interacting with the audience during a performance, they just concentrate on their music and stare down at their shoes. If you are that kind of person, you can stare at your canvas. No problem at all. But be aware, there may be as many as a few hundred spectators behind you. If you are more of a people person, you will fit right in and might even enjoy the attention. Just remember that graphic recording is not about you and your performance—it is about creating a good documentation and making the voices in the room heard.

Sometimes people in the audience near you may talk or have side conversations. It can be really hard to filter out those noises and pay attention to the speaker at the same time. People are usually very understanding if you ask them to keep quiet or take their conversation out of the room. It shows respect for your work.

Still, there is always the possibility of critical voices during or after an event. There are those who may feel that your work looks good but doesn't add anything, or who think that hand-drawn information will not be taken seriously. However, people appreciate handmade work more than you might think. In practice, people are much more open to visuals than you might expect. And while there's no conclusive research on whether hand-drawn information is taken more or less seriously, a graphic recorder's experience usually indicates that the majority of people are supportive of visuals, no matter what their background or current job is. It is important to be aware of the context of the talk. For anything process-related and dialogue-driven, graphic recording is a great tool, no matter if you are dealing with bankers and businessmen or a group of street workers. If you are going to be giving a presentation to the CEO of a Fortune 500 company, though, you should still check if graphic recording is an appropriate style. Give it a try anyway, you might be surprised! Finally, there is the question of how "sustainable" graphic recordings are. They are often criticized for not being self-explanatory—and they aren't. That is because a graphic recorder's job is to distill the meaning, not to take shorthand. It is a visual summary that supports stories, memories, and overviews, but it is not a substitution for any of them.

Pulling It All Together
—

In the end, the big challenge in graphic recording is performing all the preceding tasks at once. Especially in the beginning, this can be overwhelming. Standing in front of a crowd can add to the feeling of having too much on your hands. But as in many other creative disciplines, practitioners of graphic recording can get into "the flow" or "the zone." Flow is defined as a "mental state of operation in which a person performing an activity is fully immersed in a feeling of energized focus, full involvement, and enjoyment in the process of the activity." When you find yourself in a state of flow, all the various parts of the graphic recording just seem to come together.

If you find it difficult to get into the groove despite the preparations and advice outlined above, there are some things that may help. If you can't come up with images and visual translations right away, focus on typography and use of color. If you are worried that too many people are watching, find a place in the back of the room and present your results later. If you are uncertain whether a full-fledged graphic recording is for you, you may want to start sketchnoting, which is like graphic recording on a small scale for an audience of one—yourself. But most importantly: just start. There's really no better way to get going.

GUIDELINES AND TIPS FOR OVERCOMING CHALLENGES

- Call up a graphic recorder and ask if you can follow a day's work. Become an apprentice for a short while and it might give you the confidence to try it yourself.
- Afraid to go solo? Team up! It's lots of fun to draw together and when you're up there with someone else you can focus on what you're good at.
- Seek opportunities and find environments to practice in. Maybe call up a company you like or a friend who runs a business where you can test the waters for a graphic recording challenge.
- Chill. No, really. Relax. Graphic recording is not a job for perfectionists. Missed a quote? So what. Grab a pen. Draw away. Enjoy!

Chapter 2.3
—
How to Finish
—

While most graphic recording work is done on-site, there are also many opportunities to further develop the visual after the event is over, whether by enhancing it, creating a screencast video, or using it in other projects or workflows.

Also, most clients and participants would like to have a picture of the graphic recording, regardless of whether they take one themselves. Bring a camera, take pictures, and fine-tune your photos with Photoshop or a similar program. This is an easy way to make your analog art available digitally, which can open it up to larger audiences and new uses.
—

Post-production
—

A graphic recording is usually finished when the talk is over, but that's not necessarily the end of the process. You might want to add some elements, finish a quote that you did not have time to scribble, or add some color to create a flow in your visual. You might also want to digitize your creation, as it enables you to share it more easily with a large audience and gives you the opportunity to edit it with more detail.

Digitizing a Graphic Recording
—

Digitization is one way that you can work to cascade the learning effects, which is another way of saying that you can multiply and extend the learning effects beyond the event itself. You can do so by photographing your recording, of course, but you can also work directly in the digital realm on a tablet or a similar tool (see the next section for more about that).

Enhancing a Graphic Recording
—

Think of it as refining the image and giving it a second life. Most graphic recorders plan a little extra time after each job for finishing touches. The most common workflow is taking photos on-site and then polishing them in Photoshop (look for tutorials on YouTube). Some graphic recorders also work further on the colors to create a more even look. The visuals usually take on a more digital appearance. That can achieve a nice and clean look or lose some of its handmade charm. It's really a matter of taste.

Presentations
—

Graphic recordings are often used in contexts other than the event itself. Digitizing the visuals is only the first step—the second is finding pieces in your graphic recording that can be reused,

like symbols, icons, characters, etc. These make great slides for presentations.

Networking and Connecting
—

A graphic recording can be used long after the event is over for sharing information and knowledge with colleagues (either by showing the original piece or a digital copy). This can give further momentum to the event itself and enable the content to have a physical presence (by putting the graphic recording in a prominent place where people pass by and can have a look). Besides benefitting the participants and hosts, it can also be a way for you to increase your exposure. By connecting to Behance and other online communities, you can publish directly to your online portfolio, which makes it possible to get feedback on your visuals from your network or community. The post-talk period is a great opportunity to

chat with people about your work. There will usually be someone in the audience who was captivated by the graphic recording and who wants to take a look or snap a picture or two. With that in mind, feel free to invite people to take a closer look. Ask them what they heard or what they particularly like about your drawing. If the speaker stops by you might want to ask whether or how well you captured their main thoughts.

Screencast Videos
—

If you have taken the fully digital route (see below), there are apps and software that make it possible to screencast the drawing as it happens on your tablet. Others offer the simpler option of exporting the drawing as a video. This is a really nice add-on to have and can bring a graphic recording to life when it is shared after an event. It is also a great way to combine a graphic recording and other visual content. Think of slideshows, video summaries, and documentaries.

Chapter 2.4
—
Beyond Paper: Digital Graphic Recording
—

So far we have discussed what we can call analog graphic recording. And that offline, tactile approach has many advantages, as we've noted: there are no technological distractions, it has a continuous presence (no need to plug in a screen or keep a computer running), and it really plays up the appealing aspects of craftsmanship. But we've also discussed ways that even offline, analog graphic recordings can be enhanced, shared, or made more useful via various technologies—like making videos or taking photos for sharing, adding QR codes to direct people to additional information, etc. It is important to know that digital graphic recording is also an interesting option thanks to the rise of affordable and portable devices like the iPad or Microsoft Surface. You'll lose that sense of intimacy that comes from pen and paper, but you'll also gain several advantages.
—

What Is Digital Graphic Recording?
—

A digital graphic recording (or DGR) is pretty much what it sounds like—a graphic recording produced digitally. This usually involves drawing digitally on some kind of tablet, screen, or similar device that is connected to a large monitor or projector. Even though pen and paper are no longer involved, the live performance aspects remain the same. The new focus on hardware and software opens up both new possibilities and new challenges—and the field is continually evolving.

Advantages of Digital Graphic Recording
—

- DGR offers flexibility in editing your work after the event.
- Large variety of software and devices to choose from.
- Creatives used to working on desktop applications like SketchBook Pro or Adobe Creative Suite can easily apply those skills in a graphic recording setting.
- DGR makes distribution simple: it's easy to export, upload, and share images.

Challenges of Digital Graphic Recording
—

- With endless possibilities, it is also important to stay focused while working live: quick access to in-app tools like brushes, erasers, layers, and opacity is crucial.
- Apps sometimes crash or malfunction—especially in a live setting, you need a reliable solution.
- A lot of apps are not continuously developed. You might pick a favorite, only to find out that it will not be updated.
- TIP: Focus on apps that have a good number of reviews and that seem to be under continual development.

When It Makes Sense to Go Digital
—

While we recommend analog graphic recording in most situations, there are some cases where it makes sense to go digital. For instance, when you have bigger crowds where only people in the first couple of rows can see what is drawn—a DGR can be put on a larger screen. If you need to be able to choose between zooming in on specific details and displaying the picture as a whole, DGR is your best option. And if the graphic recording is only part of the deliverable, and the visuals are going to be digitally enhanced afterwards for further use in other mediums, then DGR offers more possibilities than AGR for high-resolution pictures and moving images.

Standard Tools for Digital Graphic Recording
—

The main tools for DGR are Apple iPads, Microsoft Surfaces, and Wacom Pen Displays, all of which are used for drawing on and each of which has different software solutions available for it. You will also likely want to use a stylus for better control of the lines you are drawing. And it is worth looking into online whiteboards, which run in the browser and so can be used and shared on any device.

Apple
The iPad Pro is an especially powerful platform due to its size (large drawing area), processing power, and depth-touch capability (its screen is sensitive to how hard you press on it). In general, Apple's line of iPads also has the advantage of being a very popular software platform, so there is a large variety of apps that are designed or optimized for iPads (rather than being ported from other platforms) and that are often available for iOS before other platforms or even exclusive to it.

Microsoft Surface
The Surface 3 and similar editions runs full software like Adobe Photoshop or SketchBook Pro as well as apps. It is about as big as a sheet of paper. It comes with a stylus that is fitted to the device. And it can quickly and easily transform into a laptop if the need arises.

Wacom Pen Display
Wacom Pen Displays run full software like Adobe Photoshop or SketchBook Pro and allow you to work directly on the screen with a pressure-sensitive pen. Multi-touch possibilities are also available. The devices come in various sizes and the rotating stand can be adjusted to your preferred working position.

Online Whiteboards
Online whiteboards offer the possibility to create quick and rough sketches within a browser, regardless of which device you are using. The toolbars they provide are not as extensive as those of native apps, but they are adequate for sketching.

Online whiteboards are where DGR really begins to open up new possibilities because they support co-creation, meaning that multiple artists can work on the same project at the same time. Others can watch as the visual takes shape.

Screen sharing displays what's happening on your screen to a wider audience. This is usually done on a laptop or a desktop computer and can also provide audio along with the visual. It is a practical solution if you're already comfortable with certain software on your computer and want to try out DGR with familiar software.

Stylus
A stylus is a pen-shaped tool for writing on screens. An alternative to using your finger, it offers a greater degree of control and most graphic recorders use them. A standard stylus with a rubber tip and no Bluetooth will work with all touch devices. They are relatively inexpensive, work with all apps, and are a good way to get started with a stylus. Some apps and companies have developed special styluses for their own products—which sometimes work with other apps or devices, and sometimes don't. Pressure-sensitive styluses like Adobe Ink, Pencil by 53, and styluses from Adonit and Wacom for the iPad as well as other tablets and smart-phones offer even more precision and control. They connect directly to the app via Bluetooth. The Apple Pencil for the iPad Pro also runs via Bluetooth—it's a game changer.

Useful App Features
Apps offer a variety of features like:

- Video capture: Allows you to export a video of your drawing.
- Vector- or pixel-based: Choose the style you need and like.
- Layers: Usually both photo and drawing layers, which makes it possible to create complexity, depth, and dimensionality.
- Manipulation: It is often also possible to duplicate, merge, flip, scale, and adjust opacity.
- Toolbars: You can organize favorite tools, brushes, and colors in a toolbar for quick access during live drawing.
- Presets: Some apps offer shapes, stamps, and stencils that can be inserted into the drawings from a library.
- Automatic shape recognition: Other apps correct free-drawn shapes like circles or squares into proper geometric shapes. This predictive technology speeds up the creation of diagrams, charts, and presentation sketches.
- Split screen: The audience only sees an image of the graphic recording itself, rather than the tools on the graphic recorder's screen or the zooming in and out that occurs during the drawing process.

- Hand recognition: You can rest your hand on the surface while drawing without the app thinking you're tying to make a mark.
- Perspective and grids: These make it easy to align elements in drawings and create a sense of perspective.

Setup for Digital Graphic Recording
—

The setup for a digital graphic recording is slightly different than for an analog one. The graphic recorder will either be standing or sitting while drawing. When sitting, it's important to find a comfortable position to draw in since you'll be hunched over, staring at the device all day. Using a stand may help you avoid neck pain. Some devices come with one, or you can build your own. If the DGR will not be visible to the audience while you're working, there are only a few things you need to consider. Make sure you're near an outlet if you need to charge your device—and that you fully charge it the night before. Find yourself a comfortable spot to sit or stand where you can hear well.

If the drawing is going to be visible to the audience while you work, there are a few more matters to attend to. One is the size of the screen: in most apps, all the action is visible on the second display, including accessing the toolbar and zooming in and out. If too much is going on, onlookers may get dizzy. The larger the screen, the more difficult it will be to watch. Consider using an app that has a "follow mode" that won't mirror your movements on the second screen.

Always plan a generous amount of time for a tech check in advance. You'll need to begin making technical arrangements well before the event, but even on-site there are many variables at play, with various workflows and technical setups to account for. It is better to be overprepared.

Another thing to consider before you start is the length of the session in relation to the size of your canvas and how much you are able to zoom in and out. Apps offer different canvas sizes and zooming options. The longer the talk, the larger the canvas should be and the more ability to zoom you'll need.

Lastly, ensure that you have quick access to your tools. Make sure you know your hardware and software inside out. Graphic recording is all about being quick. And not looking for the right swipe or scroll can save you time you can spend on listening and drawing instead.

How DGR Differs from AGR
—

Despite being based on the same basic principles, digital graphic recording can be very different from its analog cousin. For instance, the size of the canvas is highly variable and you can only see close-up details or an overview on your tablet screen. It is easy to get lost on a digital canvas because you almost never have the big picture in front of you like you do in an analog graphic recording. You'll need to zoom in and out constantly, which will take some time to get used to. Since you'll have so many options at your fingertips, you will also need to make an effort to ensure that your design elements are coherent. You'll find yourself asking if the brushstroke is the same one you used before, if the heading is the same size, etc.

DGR also demands a different kind of visual thinking. In a digital graphic recording you can work in layers easily, which can create great effects overall. It is much simpler to work with negative space. Fill out large forms with color and work with an eraser or lighter colors on top.

Going digital also shakes up the aesthetics. Pixel-based apps have a look and feel similar to that of analog graphic recording—but it's still easy for a trained eye to spot the difference between pen on paper and pen on screen. Vector-based apps, on the other hand, have a noticeably different look and feel.

Remember that one large benefit of analog graphic recording—that the audience can watch the drawing take shape—is not always available with digital graphic recording. If you're not connected to a screen, you won't be able to share the process. And if your device is connected to the main screen, it will often be in conflict with other screen-worthy content, like presentation slides or the speaker himself/herself. One way to avoid this is to have a camera crew who can switch between different channels, or maybe even a split screen, both of which will allow you to balance all the visual input for the audience.

10 TIPS FOR DIGITAL GRAPHIC RECORDING

1. Can't decide on an app? Define what's most important for the outcome (high-res image, video capability, a certain style) and choose the app accordingly.

2. There's no perfect app for graphic recorders—know your needs and find an app that suits them.

3. Once you find an app you like and that covers your needs, get to know it really well.

4. Know all the shortcuts.

5. Have your color palette ready in your app.

6. Prepare a set of preset brushes that you always have access to in your app.

7. Plan an extra hour before the event to test the equipment on-site.

8. Make sure your device is fully charged. And if you have a second device, bring it just in case.

9. Bring all the connectors, cables, and chargers you might need.

10. Choose an app you're comfortable with, then try out styluses. Not all pens work with each app and vice versa.

Chapter 3
—
Graphic Recording at Work: How to Use Graphic Recording in Your Company and How to Become a Graphic Recorder Yourself
—

By now you know why graphic recording is such an interesting and powerful tool, and you know the nuts and bolts of how to produce a graphic recoding. But how can you actually get started making graphic recordings yourself? And how would you go about introducing graphic recording to your workflow and using it in your company or organization? Read on!
—

I Want To Become A Graphic Recorder
—

Getting started with graphic recording is not as difficult as you may think. Making the transition from your first sketchnotes to a full-fledged graphic recording might take some practice, but if you have an interest in learning, visualizing, or just getting better at memorizing, you can easily pick up some techniques that will set you on the path towards becoming a visual thinker and, eventually, a graphic recorder.

Dispelling Doubts
—

First, let's dispel the notion that you need to be a creative person in order to do something like graphic recording. Even if you do not feel artsy, picking up a pen and starting to doodle can quickly become your thing. Every book you will read on this topic—including this one right here—will tell you that graphic recording, sketchnoting, visual thinking, and their ilk are not about art. And that's the truth. Graphic recording is about communication.

And since the core of graphic recording is communication and not art, all you need to get started is a basic visual vocabulary. Simple drawings will help you get your point across—in fact, simple drawings are all you ever really need. So while artistic talent is certainly helpful, it is not a prerequisite. And you can always do exercises to improve specific skills.

Easy Ways To Improve Core Skills
—

If you are ready to take the plunge, there are four skills that you will need to be aware of and possibly develop. You'll recognize them from the how-to section: listening, synthesizing, imagining, and drawing.

You don't need to sign up for a special course to develop these core skills. But like sports or playing a musical instrument or anything else you'd like to get good at, there are a few small exercises that you can do just about anywhere, anytime, to improve your abilities.

Three Ways to Improve Your Listening Skills
Listening may come to us naturally, but getting better at it is all about the approach you take.
1. Every once in a while, just listen to conversations rather than participating.
2. Listen actively, with focus and purpose, to a speech or presentation. No distractions.
3. Listen for and take note of metaphors, key words, structure, emotions, and things "that stick."

fig. 1 (opposite page)
It's time for peace! –
Geneva Peace Talks 2015
(peacetalks.net), at United
Nations Office at Geneva
UN Photo/Jean-Marc Ferré
Graphic Recording/Gabriele
Schlipf – momik*
–

Three Ways to Improve Your Synthesizing Skills

"Synthesizing" sounds serious, but it is a fundamental skill that you have many chances to practice in everyday life.

1. Watch longer talks or conversations, like current affairs discussion programs or conference talks that are posted online.
2. Make mental notes while listening.
3. After the talk is over, write down the main points that stuck in your mind.

Three Ways to Improve Your Imagining Skills

Who knew that daydreaming would one day come in handy?

1. Doodle while listening—during phone conversations, for instance.
2. Doodle on magazines and newspapers as you read or browse them.
3. Train your mind's eye by actively imagining words that you hear.

Three Ways to Improve Your Drawing Skills

These tips are just slightly more involved than the others because you'll need to get better at drawing in ways that specifically relate to graphic recording.

1. Build a visual vocabulary. If you've ever learned another language, you know that before being able to speak full sentences, you start by learning individual words. The same strategy can help you learn graphic recording. Start a collection of words and translate them into simple images. This will expand your visual vocabulary and help you speak in a visual language. Do speed drills if you want to get faster.
2. Create doodle moments. We talked about doodling to help your imagination—this is a more goal-oriented exercise where you should try to quickly draw specific things within a specific time frame. For instance, you can get in the habit of doing things like sketching your family's weekly grocery list or just drawing a smiley picture or icon every day.
3. Find your favorite drawing tool. You like markers? You love gadgets? Great! Having a tool that you think is fun to work with will encourage you to draw more often, and make doing so more enjoyable.

If you already have one or more of these skills, then go ahead and give graphic recording a try. Diving in is usually the best way to get started. Small-scale sketchnotes might be a good format to work with in the beginning. You can slowly progress and master the other skills along the way while also trying out new formats. You will notice that with more practice you will gain confidence and automatically start to explore new things.

The preceding suggestions will help you get started, but if you outgrow them, there's a whole world of tutorials available online. Check sites like YouTube and lynda.com or just search for "learn graphic recording" and you will find plenty of links to additional exercises and lessons.

Making Connections in the World of Graphic Recordings
—

While you can learn and practice graphic recording on your own, it will be easier to make progress if you connect with "the guild." Besides being able to provide helpful feedback, other graphic recorders and professional organizations and associations will be able to direct you to resources, help you network, and even help you find your first clients if you are considering a freelance career.

If you learn well by watching and sharing experiences with others, there are plenty of opportunities to connect with other graphic recorders around the world, and maybe even in your country too (depending on where you live). The most important are the IFVP, conferences, local and online communities, and online courses.

The IFVP is the International Forum for Visual Practitioners. It offers a website, an online community, and a directory. In order to access the community, though, you will need a membership. The IVFP also hosts an annual conference at a different location each year. Check the website for the new date. It is usually held in the summer.

No matter where you are in the world, you are likely to find meetups for visual thinking or even specifically for graphic recording. Meetup.com is a good place to look internationally. You may also find country-specific sites that organize meetups—for instance, vizthink.de organizes regular meetings all over Germany. An online search using key words like visual thinking, sketchnotes, or graphic recording plus your country or region will quickly yield results.

If you cannot make it to a face-to-face meetup, there are still many online communities that you can participate in. The current place to meet right now is a Facebook group called Graphic Facilitation. It is an active group with members from all over the world. Questions are asked, answers are given, and a lot of work is shared by both beginners and professionals. Some of those professionals also offer online courses. Lasting anywhere from a day to a few weeks, they represent good ways to learn more about the craft in a structured environment.

Wherever you are, whatever your skill level, don't be afraid to reach out. As long as you are respectful, you should be able to find a place in the graphic recording community.

Using Graphic Recording in Your Organization
—

Perhaps you want to use graphic recording for a meeting, conference, or workshop. You will not be doing the recording yourself—maybe you will be a participant, or maybe you are responsible for organizing the event. In that case, you don't need to worry about building skills, but you will need to consider some organizational issues. To plan a good graphic recording experience, think of three stages: before, during, and after the event.

What to Consider Before the Event
—

In the run-up to the event you will need to consider the purpose, logistics, and content—and you will need to hire a graphic recorder.

Deciding on the Purpose of Your Event
Thinking about why you would hire a graphic recorder and knowing your goals will help you in the planning process. The first question you ask yourself should always be: what is the purpose of recording your discussion? This will also help the graphic recorder do a better job. They can suggest appropriate formats, styles, and setups. For this, get the scribe on board as soon as possible. They can contribute with meaningful experience and suggestions.

Examples of good purposes include: "I'd like people to enjoy an artistic performance" (experience), "We'd like people to remember what has been talked about for months to come" (document), or "We'd like to create a visual style for our upcoming change process and would like to use graphic recording as a kick-off" (tool).

Figuring Out the Logistics
Talk about the logistics with your graphic recorder in advance. How big should the drawing area be? Should people see what is being drawn? Which parts should be recorded? Analog or digital? And—how would you like to share the results afterwards? Your graphic recorder will likely ask about many of the important details, but you should also create a checklist with all the questions you might have.

Clearing Up the Content
You should also spend some time establishing the key elements of the content. The graphic recorder does not need to become an expert in your field. After all, they are there for the big picture and not the details. But a bit of insight, especially if there are lots of abbreviations or jargon in your line of work, does not hurt. Going through the agenda together is usually a good way to brief your scribe.

Hiring the Right Graphic Recorder

Of course, you cannot finalize the logistics and deliver a briefing about the content until you have a graphic recorder on board. So how can you find the right one?

One place to start the search is among your acquaintances. Graphic recording has been around for a while and most likely one of your friends, colleagues, or business connections already has experience hiring one. Reach out to them—direct recommendations are often helpful and trustworthy. If that does not result in a suitable candidate, do some research online. Most graphic recorders have a web presence. You can browse through portfolios and websites to get inspired. You will also be able to access directories and online communities. Networks like the IFVP or Facebook groups focusing on graphic recording give you easy access to artists all over the world.

As you are evaluating the possible candidates, keep the following three factors in mind: style, availability, and formal requirements.

Evaluating a Scribe's Style

If you do not have a lot of experience with graphic recording, different artists' styles may look similar to you. Spend some time looking at portfolios to choose the kind of style you like. Do you prefer a balance between text and images? Is it important to you that the graphic recording be colorful? Do you like character-driven visuals? Think about what suits your event.

Determining Availability

Graphic recorders are often in high demand, especially during "high season" in the spring and fall. Remember that it's not just the day of the event that matters—depending on the type of event, the subject matter, and other requirements you might have, the graphic recorder may need time before the event to prepare or after the event for post-production work. You should let potential graphic recorders know in advance if you will need pre-drawn materials or a video of the graphic recording process, etc.

Formal Requirements for Your Scribe

Your event might have formal requirements like:
- A foreign language.
- An off-site location requiring significant travel time.
- The need for the graphic recorder to be able to support graphic facilitation and team up with a facilitator.
- The need for a digital graphic recording during the event, or an enhanced digital version afterwards.

Your requirements will often narrow down the choice of graphic recorders, which will help you find an artist who has all the skills you seek and ensure that they really suit your needs.

What to Watch Out For During the Event
—

You've found a graphic recorder whose style you like and who will be joining your event? Wonderful! You're off to a good start. So what else should you think of during the event? The way that the graphic recording will be used. Specifically, your graphic recording will be used for some combination of documentation, experience, and entertainment.

Graphic Recordings for Documentation

Graphic recording is a powerful tool on its own. But it is also a good team player. Think of coupling graphic recording with other forms of visual documentation, like photography or a video. The result could be a split screen presentation where both the graphic recording and the speaker are shown. Or a short documentary sent out after the event. Or slideshows and pictures of the speakers with the graphic recording. There are several options.

Use graphic recording as a photo opportunity for the audience and also those who are not participating. If you are running a big event, think about creating a hashtag for the graphic recording. Then people will be able it find it easily on social media like Facebook, Instagram, or Twitter. If it is a closed meeting, send out pictures to your colleagues either as documentation afterwards or as a status update in between.

Graphic Recordings for Experience and Entertainment

Clients often express a fear that the audience will be distracted by the graphic recording—that "everyone will just look at the amazing drawing and not listen to the speakers." Yet if they are asked, most of the people watching will say that they are not distracted, but instead that they pay more attention to the overall messages of both the talk and the drawing. Trust your audience and let people see the drawing as it grows. It enhances rather than distracts and can be a memorable process to watch.

Brief the audience and let them know what graphic recording is. Something along the line of "we have a graphic recorder joining us today who will help us capture the content and atmosphere of our event" will do in a pinch. Also encourage the audience to take a closer look during the breaks. People love to take pictures—use the graphic recording as a prop for them to engage with the content.

Let the speaker and the graphic recorder work together, not as rivals. Talk to the speaker beforehand to verify that it is okay with them that someone will be drawing while they are talking, and talk about what good positioning within the room could be. Speakers usually love having their talks drawn. It shows appreciation for their effort and performance.

THE END IS ONLY THE BEGINNING: WHAT TO DO WITH YOUR GRAPHIC RECORDING AFTER THE EVENT

Giving a graphic recording away—to the speaker or a participant, for instance—can be a very good idea. It is an act of appreciation—one that is often unexpected, but always appreciated. There will often be someone who asks what happens to the original, and they may be exactly the person who should get to take it home or bring it back to their office. That being said, you can also keep it for yourself, of course. Graphic recordings make for nice office decorations, and clients with regular events have small galleries showing off their previous graphic recordings.

GRAPHIC RECORDINGS FOR KNOWLEDGE MANAGEMENT

Goal: Cascading knowledge
Useful for:

- Introducing new strategies.
- Rolling out plans.
- Retrospectives.
- Simply sharing what has been talked about without getting everyone together in a room or organizing a second follow-up discussion.

REUSING GRAPHIC RECORDINGS

Parts of the image can be reused for:

- Presentations.
- Other media like websites or brochures.
- As an aid to implementing the visual style.
- Or even for creating merchandise.

After the Event
—

A graphic recording is a great tool for retelling what has happened. Later viewers can choose how much time to spend with it and how deeply to dive in. Place the graphic recording somewhere where many people can see it, like a central location or a place where people stop or congregate (the coffee machine or water fountain, for instance). It will serve as a silent yet engaging reminder. But a graphic recording is not like a comic strip that retells the whole conference by itself. Think of it as a guide or a map that will help you do a better job of relating the story afterwards.

If you'd like to have a self-explanatory visual that viewers can interpret without reference to the original talk or presentation, talk to your graphic recorder about developing one afterwards. Visuals are often further developed into learning maps, movies, or graphic elements for presentations.

THREE EASY WAYS TO CREATE A MORE VISUAL WORKPLACE

- Hire a graphic recorder. It is not only easy, it is effective: in the end, you will have results to show for it.

- Set up your space to facilitate visuals. Doing so does not require a large investment. Buy a bag of markers, a whiteboard or flipchart, or go big and paint a whole wall with whiteboard paint.
- Organize a workshop on visual thinking. Treat yourself and your team to a day of fun, creative thinking—and build up your visual skills in the process.

So You've Tried Graphic Recording and Now You Want More
—

After having worked with graphic recordings, many people are inspired to do more. Keeping that creative spark lit is not all that difficult—you can naturally progress to other ways of thinking and communicating visually.

MAKING YOUR MEETINGS INTO VISUAL MEETINGS

- Have your sticky notes, markers, and drawing surfaces (like paper, whiteboards, and flipcharts) ready. This makes working visually a lot easier.
- Are your meeting rooms equipped properly? Consider a shopping trip to kick-start your visual culture.
- Introduce visual warm-up exercises in your meetings. Little games like graphic jams can help you and your team build up visual skills in a fun and meaningful way.

Graphic recording can be the gateway to other ways of working visually. In particular, you can progress from graphic recording to graphic facilitation, which is an even more engaged use of live drawing to actively shape, guide, or help along a talk, meeting, or discussion. If you have tried out graphic recording and would like visual thinking to become an integral part of your business processes, graphic facilitation can be a good next step. It will help you use visuals in a more interactive way and enable you to embed

them in your process. Think about which of your company's current processes (they could be anything from meetings to team retreats or strategy sessions) could benefit from visuals. Redesign your processes or set up new ones together with a graphic facilitator. Start working with templates and graphic guides, and train your facilitators to become graphic facilitators.

Establishing a Visual Culture in Your Company or Team

So, how can you initiate a visual culture?

- Basic trainings for your employees are not only fun, they are good kick-starters for spreading visual thinking within your company.
- Pay attention to who really enjoys sketching and who continues to use it at work. Find your doodlers, then encourage and support them.
- Once you have found your visual people, consider a train-the-trainer-program. Set up a team of visual thinkers inside your company. They can continue to spread visual thinking in the company by hosting lunch sessions on sketching, organizing visual meetings, and establishing doodling as a normal way to shape ideas. Make them ambassadors.

If you need help convincing your company to spend money on training visually, consider the benefits. Participants gain more than just the ability to communicate and express themselves visually. Learning to do so also often enhances a person's strategic thinking. They will be better equipped to understand and communicate ideas, concepts, strategies, and processes.

A Concluding Thought
—

"Close to 50% of our entire brain capacity is focused on vision. Our brain consumes more energy than any other organ in our body. You put those two together and it tells you that vision is hyper critical to our survival. As humans, we are essentially visual creatures. We have lots of other senses, but central to all of them is the power of vision. Pictures enable us to take advantage of that. It would be foolish for anybody who has a message to deliver not to take advantage of that capacity for visual understanding."
— Dan Roam, IFVP interview

Chapter 4
—
Portfolio:
Examples of
Graphic Recording
—

In this section, you'll find a diverse range of
graphic recordings from all over the world.
The featured companies vary in location, size,
and industry, yet they have all understood
the benefits of graphic recording and see the
visual technique as an asset to their professional undertakings. Flip these pages to see
innovative examples of graphic recordings
alongside valuable insight into the process
from the graphic recorders themselves.
—

fig. 1   fig. 2 (opposite page)

VISUAL SCRIBING
—

visualscribing.com

-

Goudhurst & Kilndown school called Visual Scribing to create a huge mural on a massive white wall as a way of expressing their core values and how they are perceived by parents

and children. The topic of the project was the most interesting aspect; a forest school where kids interact with nature and take care of animals during school time. The visual style of the piece captures the playful and joyful nature of the topic. It reads like a big tapestry filled with little stories and a big narrative and is something that makes both kids and teachers look for details in the illustration. The basis of the characters are chunks of color that, together with the outlines, create an interesting visual effect. The time frame for the recording was very tight with only eight hours to talk to the teachers, get an idea of what the forest school is all about, and draw the entire illustration on the wall.

—

DRAWING ON SCHOOL WALLS
fig. 1–2

Client: Goudhurst & Kilndown school
Produced in: United Kingdom, 2014
Technique: Analog
Format: Workshop
Dimensions: 2 x 4 m
Time: 8 hours

—

NEVER STOP LEARNING EVENT
fig. 3

Client: Never Stop Learning
Produced in: United Kingdom, 2014
Technique: Analog
Format: Keynote
Dimensions: 3 x 1.5 m
Time: 2 hours

GRAPHIC RECORDING NETWORK BERLIN

—

Sophia Halamoda
Gabriele Heinzel
Marie Jacobi
Michael Schrenk

—

sophiahalamoda.com

gabriele-heinzel.com

visualrecording.de

liveillustration.de

—

Solve for X is a global community founded to highlight scientific innovation and technological breakthroughs that have the potential to solve problems facing humanity. The projects they tackle, known as moonshots, are defined as outlier solutions for complex problems that are enabled by science or technology. Google, which started hosting Solve for X events in 2012, also helps organize community-driven events around the world.

During the first European event in Berlin in 2015, six moonshots were presented and discussed in small breakout groups by experts from around the world. Graphic recordings by Sophia Halamoda, Gabriele Heinzel, Marie Jacobi, and Michael Schrenk and six others were projected onto a wall and used to summarize outcomes. Such a large event gave the team a chance to work together and learn from one another as they got to see ten interpretations of the same topic.

The style of the recordings developed out of a collaboration between the graphic recorder and the workshop participants, with each recorder using the same technique of contrast between color and thin and thick lines for visual consistency across all recordings.

—

GOOGLE SOLVE FOR X
fig. 1–9

Client: Google Solve for X
Produced in: Berlin, Germany, 2015
Technique: Analog
Format: Keynote followed by discussion
Dimensions: 0.7 x 1 m each
Time: 1 hour each

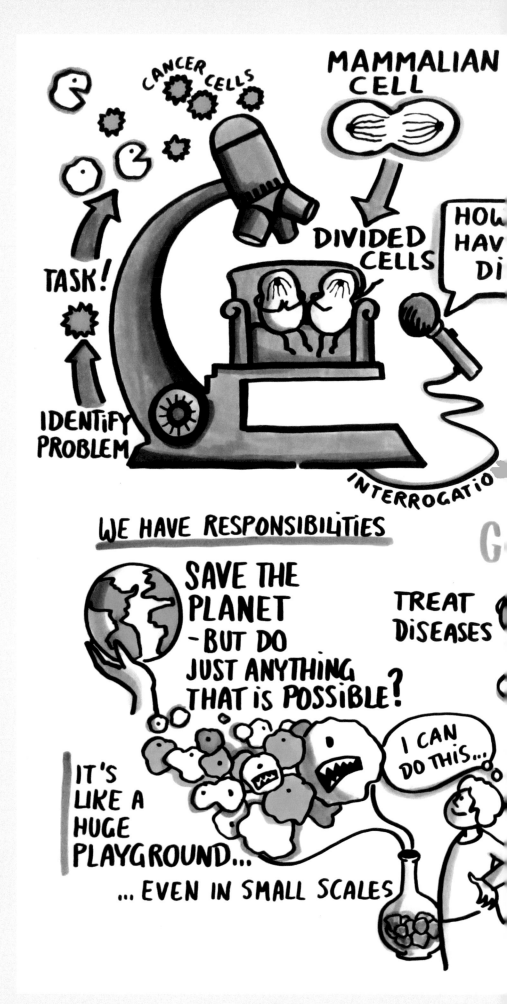

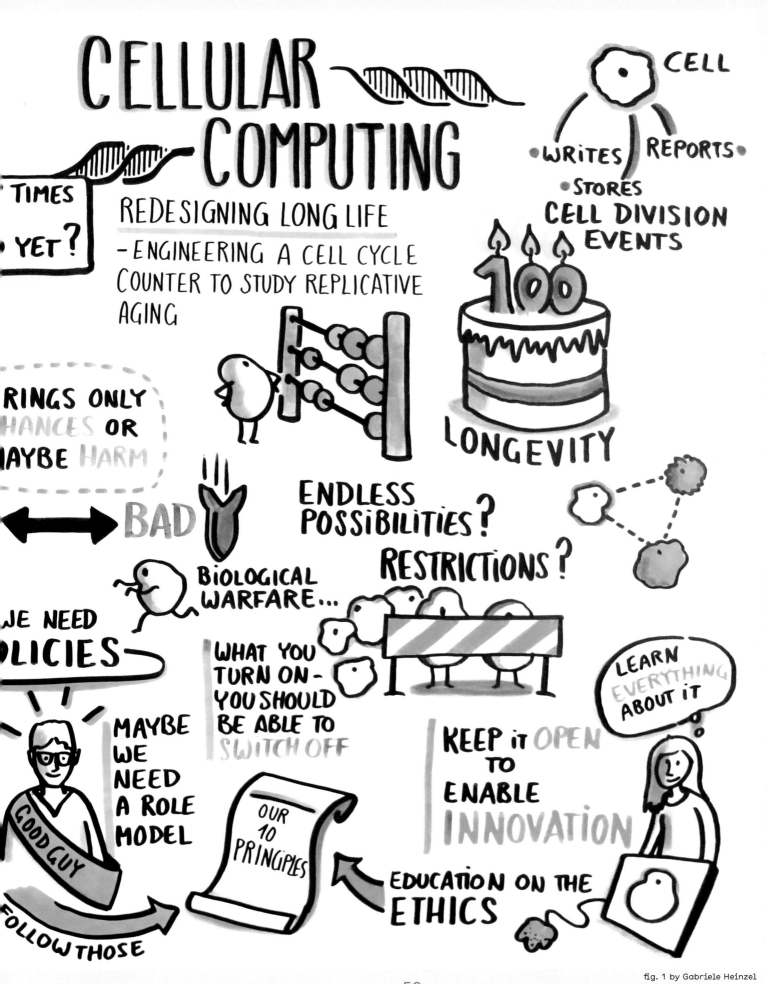

fig. 1 by Gabriele Heinzel

fig. 2 by Michael Schrenk

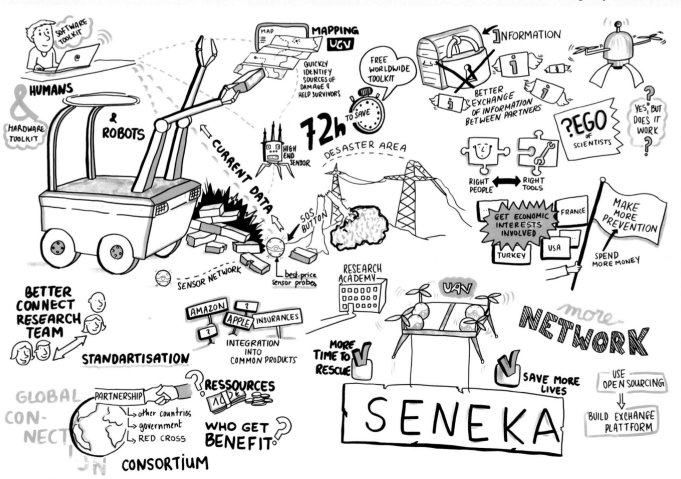

fig. 3 by Marie Jacobi

fig. 4 by Sophia Halamoda

fig. 5 by Sophia Halamoda

fig. 6 by Sophia Halamoda

fig. 7 by Gabriele Heinzel

fig. 8 by Marie Jacobi

fig. 9 by Michael Schrenk

STUDIO ANIMANOVA
—
Christoph J Kellner
—
animanova.de
—

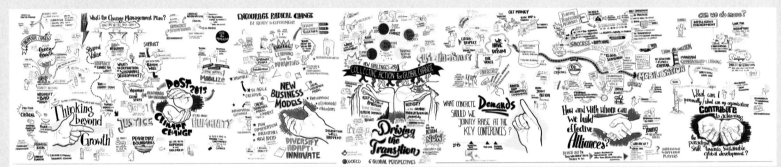

fig. 1

fig. 1
Studio Animanova's Christoph Kellner always brings the above quote by Robert Fuller on his graphic recordings because it speaks to the process.
—

One of the most challenging aspects of working as a graphic recorder is never knowing what a speaker is going to say. When working in the moment to interpret complex themes, structuring the space of the visualization is an integral part of successfully bringing all aspects of the work together.

As he planned his strategy for the International Civil Society's annual Global Perspectives conference, Christoph J Kellner drew on his background in animation and graphic design for its dynamic combination of typography, formal visual language, and visual storytelling. Kellner chose a cartooning style for both its ability to tackle serious topics with humor, charm, and humanity and because its fast gestures work well within the time constraints of a live performance. Color-coding is another important tool for strengthening the structure of a visualization.

For this piece, Kellner chose one color for each area, and then united them on the key panel in the middle.

While illustrating the themes of an event is the main goal of each recording, finding common elements to connect the themes is equally important. For Global Perspectives, which focuses on people advocating for better living and working conditions, hands became the unifying element because of their ability to create and change things for the better.

—

GLOBAL PERSPECTIVES 2014
fig. 1

Client: Civil Society Organisation
Produced in: Paris, France, 2014
Technique: Analog
Format: Keynote and Workshop
Dimensions: 1 x 5 m
Time: 16 hours

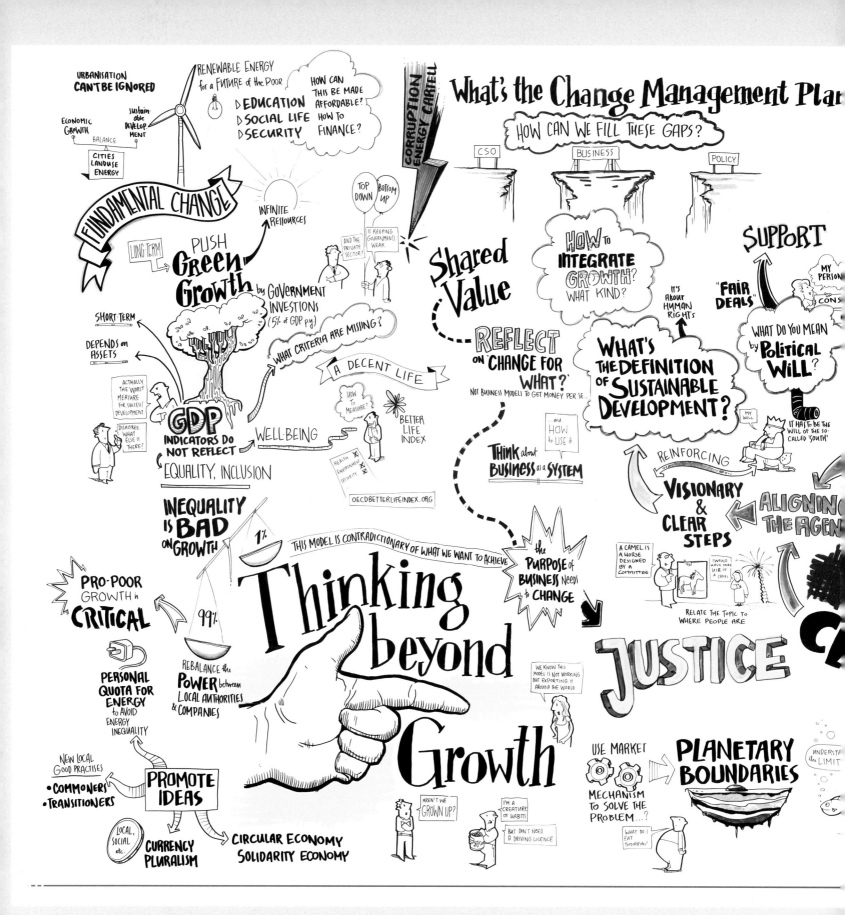

Detail zoom

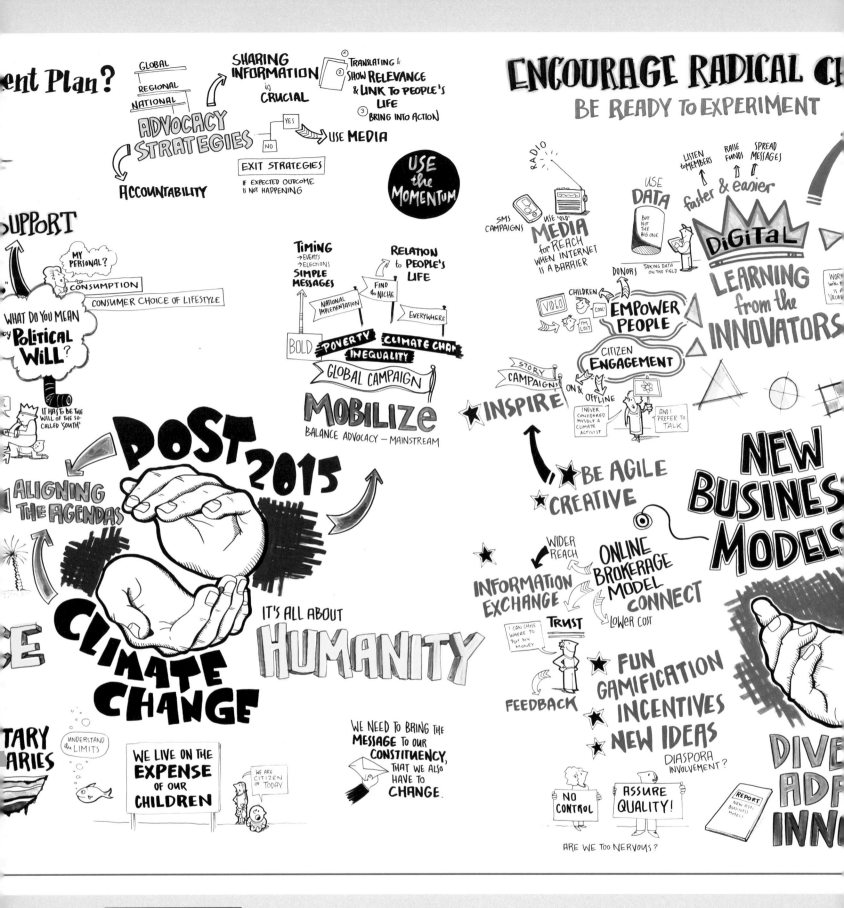

ent Plan?

GLOBAL
REGIONAL
NATIONAL

ADVOCACY STRATEGIES

Accountability

SHARING **INFORMATION** is CRUCIAL

① TRANSLATING &
② SHOW RELEVANCE & LINK TO PEOPLE'S LIFE
③ BRING INTO ACTION

YES
NO → USE MEDIA

EXIT STRATEGIES
IF EXPECTED OUTCOME IS NOT HAPPENING

USE the MOMENTUM

ENCOURAGE RADICAL C
BE READY TO EXPERIMENT

RADIO

LISTEN to MEMBERS
RAISE FUNDS
SPREAD MESSAGES

faster & easier

SMS CAMPAIGNS

USE 'OLD' **MEDIA** for REACH WHEN INTERNET IS A BARRIER

USE **DATA** BUT NOT THE BIG ONE

DIGITAL

DONORS
TAKING DATA ON THE FIELD

LEARNING from the **INNOVATORS**

WOR WITH IS A VALUE

SUPPORT

MY PERSONAL?
CONSUMPTION
CONSUMER CHOICE OF LIFESTYLE

WHAT DO YOU MEAN by **POLITICAL WILL**?

IT HAS TO BE THE WILL OF THE SO-CALLED 'SOUTH'

TIMING
→ EVENTS
→ ELECTIONS
SIMPLE MESSAGES

NATIONAL IMPLEMENTATION

BOLD
POVERTY
INEQUALITY
CLIMATE CHAN

Relation to PEOPLE'S LIFE

FIND the NICHE

EVERYWHERE

GLOBAL CAMPAIGN

MOBILIZE
BALANCE ADVOCACY — MAINSTREAM

VIDEO
CHILDREN
COOL
I'M LOST

EMPOWER PEOPLE

CITIZEN **ENGAGEMENT**

STORY **CAMPAIGNS**
ON & OFFLINE

I NEVER CONSIDERED MYSELF A CLIMATE ACTIVIST

AND I PREFER TO TALK

★ **INSPIRE**

★ **BE AGILE**
★ **CREATIVE**

NEW BUSINES MODELS

ALIGNING THE AGENDAS

POST 2015

E CLIMATE CHANGE

IT'S ALL ABOUT

HUMANITY

WIDER REACH

INFORMATION EXCHANGE

ONLINE BROKERAGE MODEL CONNECT
LOWER COST

I CAN CHOSE WHERE TO PUT MY MONEY

TRUST

FEEDBACK

★ **FUN GAMIFICATION**
★ **INCENTIVES**
★ **NEW IDEAS**

DIASPORA INVOLVEMENT?

DIVE
ADP
INN

TARY ARIES

UNDERSTAND the LIMITS

WE LIVE ON THE **EXPENSE** OF OUR **CHILDREN**

WE ARE CITIZEN OF TODAY

WE NEED TO BRING THE **MESSAGE** TO OUR **CONSTITUENCY**, THAT WE ALSO HAVE TO **CHANGE.**

NO CONTROL

ASSURE QUALITY!

REPORT
NEW IDEAS, BUSINESS MODELS

ARE WE TOO NERVOUS?

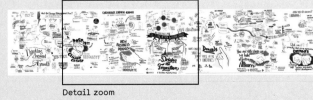
Detail zoom

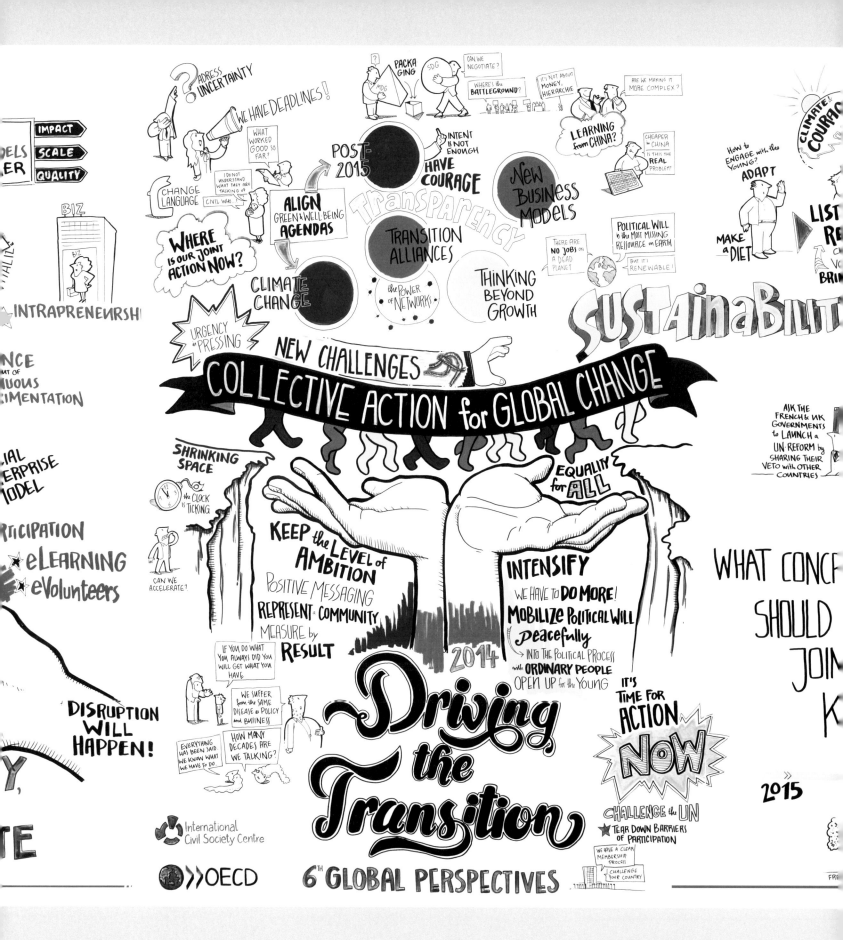

Detail zoom

68

BIGGER PICTURE

—

biggerpicture.dk

—

Each year the Re:New conference presents novel approaches to the theme of renewal. A key part of the conference concept uses visual elements to enhance conversations and give participants concrete take-aways. Bigger Picture co-designed, facilitated, and documented key elements of the conference, which were captured in a nine-meter-long visual recording that shows an overview of the event. Because the conference also aims to help the collective see a reflection of itself, Bigger Picture abandoned the typical vignette presentation. Instead, their design was experiential and helped participants see and feel the journey of the day through the eyes of two visual thinkers. With more than ten years of experience in the graphic recording field, the team has come to believe that allowing participants to contribute to the recording is extremely valuable. To do this, they listen and distill the essence of what happens in the room and record it bit by bit—a process that requires patience while meaning reveals itself and a unifying image comes forward. From there, many elements can be connected and this is what makes a recording powerful: strong visual concepts that connect with one another to form patterns. It is the patterns that are the key to visual understanding and communication.

—

RE:NEW CONFERENCE
fig. 1

Client: Re:New
Produced in: Denmark, 2014
Technique: Analog
Format: Conference
Dimensions: 1 × 9 m
Time: 9 hours

fig. 1

Detail zoom

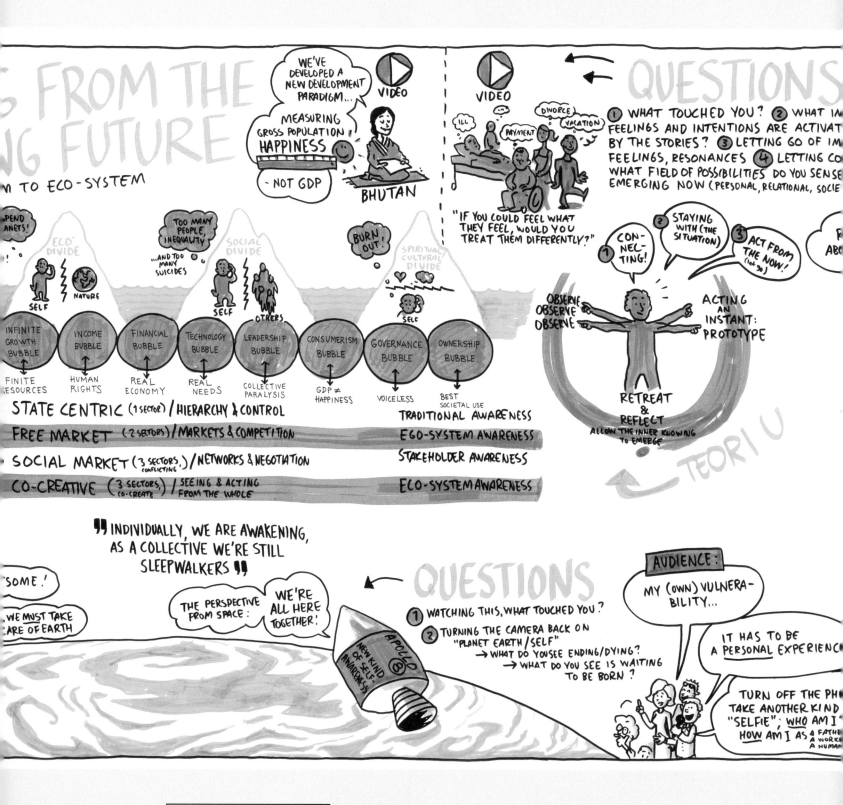

Detail zoom

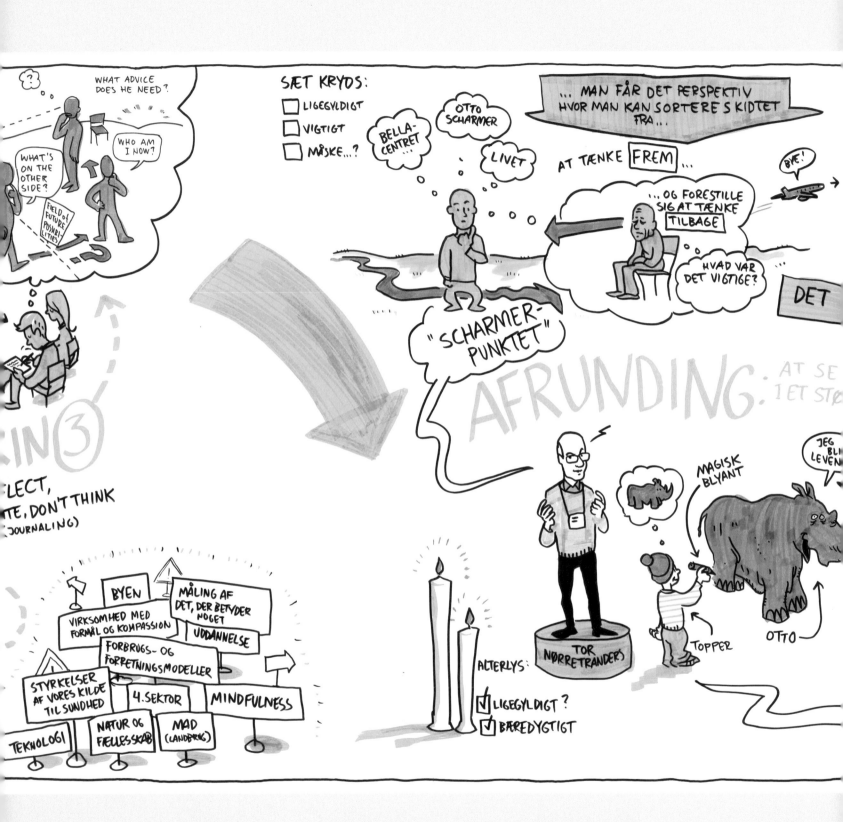

Detail zoom

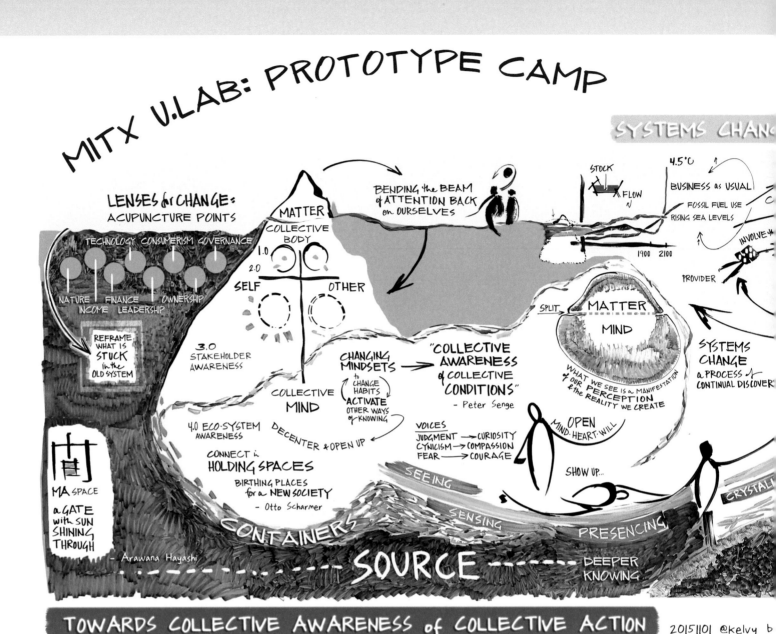

MITx U.LAB: PROTOTYPE CAMP

SYSTEMS CHAN[GE]

LENSES for CHANGE: ACUPUNCTURE POINTS

TECHNOLOGY CONSUMERISM GOVERNANCE
NATURE INCOME FINANCE LEADERSHIP OWNERSHIP

REFRAME WHAT IS STUCK in the OLD SYSTEM

MA SPACE a GATE with SUN SHINING THROUGH
— Arawana Hayashi

MATTER
COLLECTIVE BODY
1.0
2.0
SELF — OTHER

3.0 STAKEHOLDER AWARENESS
COLLECTIVE MIND
4.0 ECO·SYSTEM AWARENESS
CONNECT in HOLDING SPACES
BIRTHING PLACES for a NEW SOCIETY
— Otto Scharmer

BENDING the BEAM of ATTENTION BACK on OURSELVES

CHANGING MINDSETS to CHANGE HABITS
ACTIVATE OTHER WAYS of KNOWING
DECENTER & OPEN UP

"COLLECTIVE AWARENESS of COLLECTIVE CONDITIONS"
— Peter Senge

VOICES
JUDGMENT → CURIOSITY
CYNICISM → COMPASSION
FEAR → COURAGE

STOCK FLOW
4.5°C BUSINESS as USUAL
FOSSIL FUEL USE RISING SEA LEVELS
1900 2100
INVOLVE
PROVIDER

SPLIT
MATTER MIND
WHAT WE SEE IS a MANIFESTATION of OUR PERCEPTION & the REALITY WE CREATE

SYSTEMS CHANGE a PROCESS of CONTINUAL DISCOVER[Y]

OPEN MIND · HEART · WILL
SHOW UP...
CRYSTAL[LIZING]

SEEING
SENSING
PRESENCING
CONTAINERS
SOURCE — — — DEEPER KNOWING

TOWARDS COLLECTIVE AWARENESS of COLLECTIVE ACTION

20151101 @kelvy_b

KELVY BIRD

—

kelvybird.com

—

The ambitious u.lab Prototype Camp brought together 60 change-makers from all over the world for four intensive days of multidimensional project exploration. The challenge for the event's graphic recorder, Kelvy Bird, was to fit four days of content into a five meter space that was also needed for the presentations and participant work. Embracing a daily, iterative approach seemed to be the only possible solution. This involved drawing and erasing content each day while thoroughly documenting each round to preserve the context and the previous session.

Knowing she would have to work quickly to synthesize the large amount of content presented, Bird approached the wall as an experiment in layering by adding, subtracting, expanding, and relocating content as needed—even at the expense of completely eliminating information. Wanting to go large and aim for depth, she started with Neuland inks squeezed into marker shells meant for acrylic paint. Although it was an unusual application, the process yielded extraordinary serendipity in application and very rich color. The "secret sauce" of this image is the hand mixed dry-erase inks used to evoke potential (gold), grounding (olive), and source/spirit (blue-gray).

—

U.LAB PROTOTYPE CAMP
fig. 1

Client: MITx/Presencing Institute
Produced in: Cambridge, MA, USA, 2015
Technique: Analog
Format: Workshop
Dimensions: 4.3 x 1.2 m
Time: 20 hours over 3.5 days

—

U.LAB SOCIAL FIELDS
fig. 2

Client: MITx / Presencing Institute
Produced in: Cambridge, MA, USA, 2015
Technique: Analog
Format: Online class
Dimensions: 4.5 x 1.2 m
Time: 1.5 hours

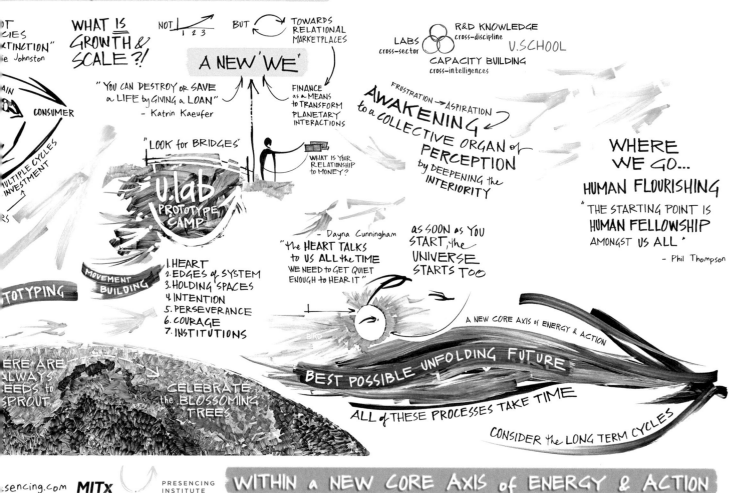

fig. 1

fig. 2

ÉDITH CARRON

—

edithcarron.net

—

For the Mehrwert Schafft Räume networking event in Berlin, graphic recorder Édith Carron recorded the keynote speech live onstage. Afterwards, a group of seven illustrators interacted with the keynote audience by listening to their reactions and bringing these ideas and questions to life in a series of visual recordings. The process resulted in a uniquely creative atmosphere during this event about the political and economic future of Berlin. Carron always uses colored pencils to do her graphic recordings because she can work quickly and with expression. They enhance her approach to the process. She sees one of the strengths of drawing to be the ability to create anything, even unrealistic images. This is an especially important quality at events such as these, where the theme of a city in the future requires images that don't exist yet. Carron also likes to use handwritten text in her work because it can both support the drawing and also contradict it, surprising the viewer and making them think twice about what they see and experience.

—

**MEHRWERT SCHAFFT RÄUME –
NETWORKING EVENT 2015**
fig. 1–6

Client: Mehrwert Berlin, eine Initiative der öffentlichen Unternehmen
Produced in: Berlin, Germany, 2015
Technique: Analog
Format: Keynote and workshop
Dimensions: 0.2 × 0.3 m
Time: Keynote: 1 hour; workshop: 2 hours

fig. 1

fig. 2

fig. 3

fig. 4

fig. 5

fig. 6

THE GRAPHIC RECORDING COMPANY

—

Alexander Czernin
Paul Tontur

—

graphic-recording.at

—

Sensitive themes like dementia and death require graphic recorders to take an empathetic approach. When working with these topics for Lebenswelt Heim, the Graphic Recording Company chose to omit humor from their work and instead focus on charming details for the images they created for the event. These visual elements, which created a specific atmosphere that encouraged the viewer to inhabit the world of people living with dementia, included an old Viennese house, a dictionary with torn-out pages to symbolize the difficulty in remembering words, and a drawing of a railway siding that referenced the neglect experienced by many with dementia. As a team of two, their process involved switching between drawing and taking notes because it allows for greater detail in the final piece. The visual language of each graphic recording is unique with a clear storyline that guarantees each event participant will easily find their contributions in the recording. Unlike other graphic recorders, the Graphic Recording Company does not draw icons repeatedly; instead, they use the landscape horizon as a connecting element. Opening the field of view in this way reduces complexity and makes the image accessible to a broader audience. When elements need emphasis, they draw them at a larger scale, with a thicker line width, or with different highlight colors.

—

EINE KULTUR DER SORGE LEBEN
fig. 1

Client: Lebenswelt Heim, Bundesverband der Alten- und Pflegeheime Österreichs
Produced in: Vienna, Austria, 2015
Technique: Analog
Format: Keynote
Dimensions: 1 x 3.5 m
Time: 12 hours

fig. 1

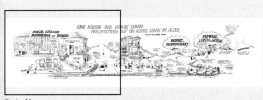

Detail zoom

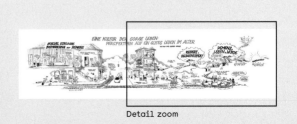

Detail zoom

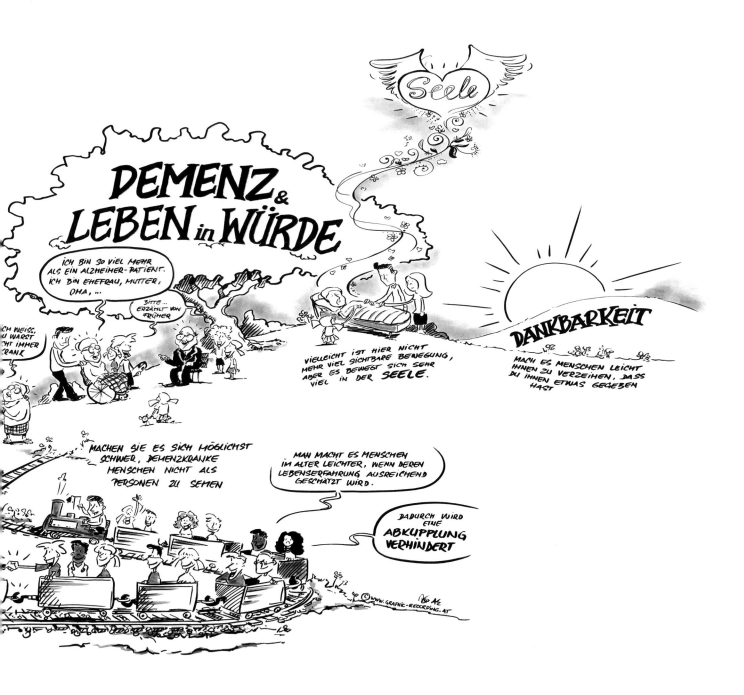

JOEL COOPER

—

joelcooper.co.uk

—

Created during the 2015 Oracle Retail
Industry Forum in Amsterdam, Joel Cooper's
graphic recording captured content from a
series of short presentations given by Oracle
as well as the contributions from the event's
Twitter feed. Although the talks were in
English, none of the audience were English
native speakers, so it was necessary to devise
a system for clear communication. The
pictographs gave the recording a distinctive
look, while elements such as the title and the
road helped to center the piece and create
a connection between speakers. To incorporate Oracle's visual identity, Cooper first
added the road and world sections. The rest
of the piece was drawn during the event.
Often called a knowledge wall, this form
of graphic recording documents the most
relevant content of a wide range of topics.

—

ORACLE RETAIL INDUSTRY FORUM
fig. 1

Client: Oracle
Produced in: Amsterdam, Netherlands, 2015
Technique: Analog
Format: Workshop
Dimensions: 2 × 1.2 m
Time: 1 day

—

THE CHANGING CONSUMER
fig. 2

Client: Platform Group
Produced in: London, United Kingdom, 2015
Technique: Analog
Format: Keynote
Dimensions: 0.84 × 1.2 m
Time: 30 minutes

—

**UNIVERSITY OF HERTFORDSHIRE -
ENHANCING CONVERSATIONS**
fig. 3

Client: University of Hertfordshire
Produced in: Hatfield, United Kingdom, 2015
Technique: Analog
Format: Workshop
Dimensions: 1.4 × 1.05 m
Time: Half-day

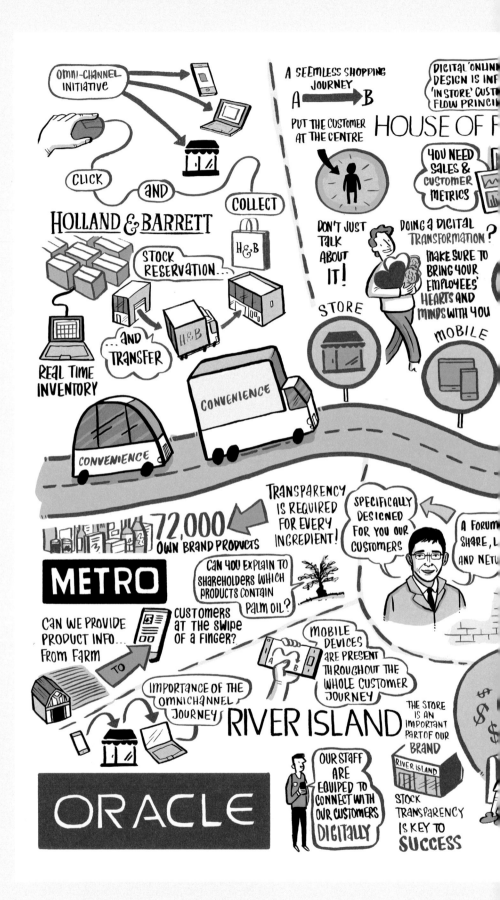

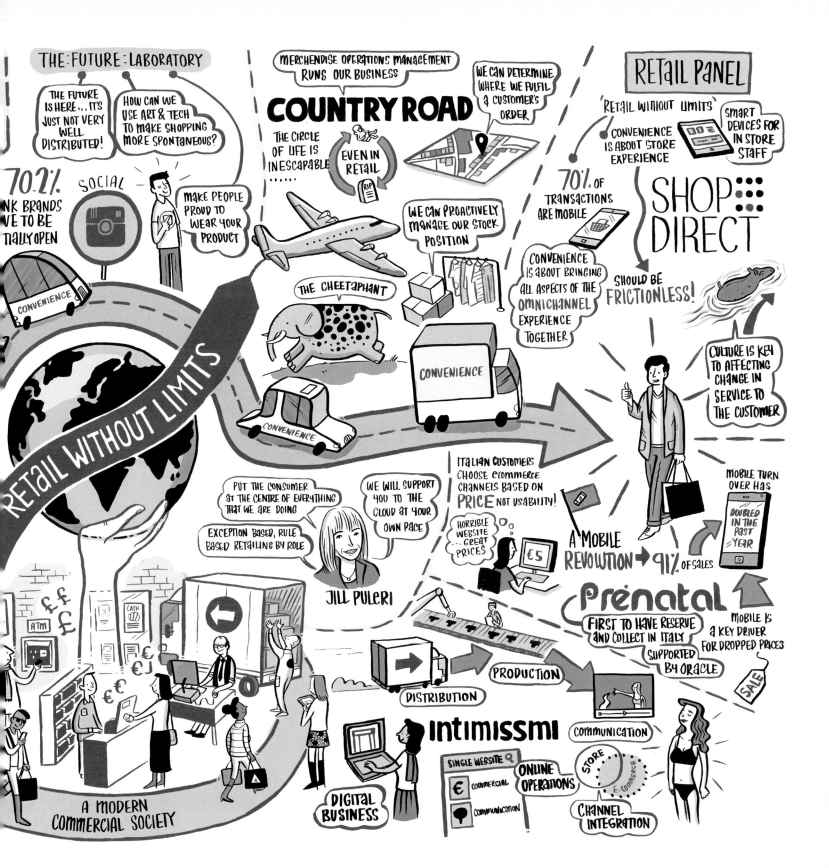

fig. 1

fig. 2

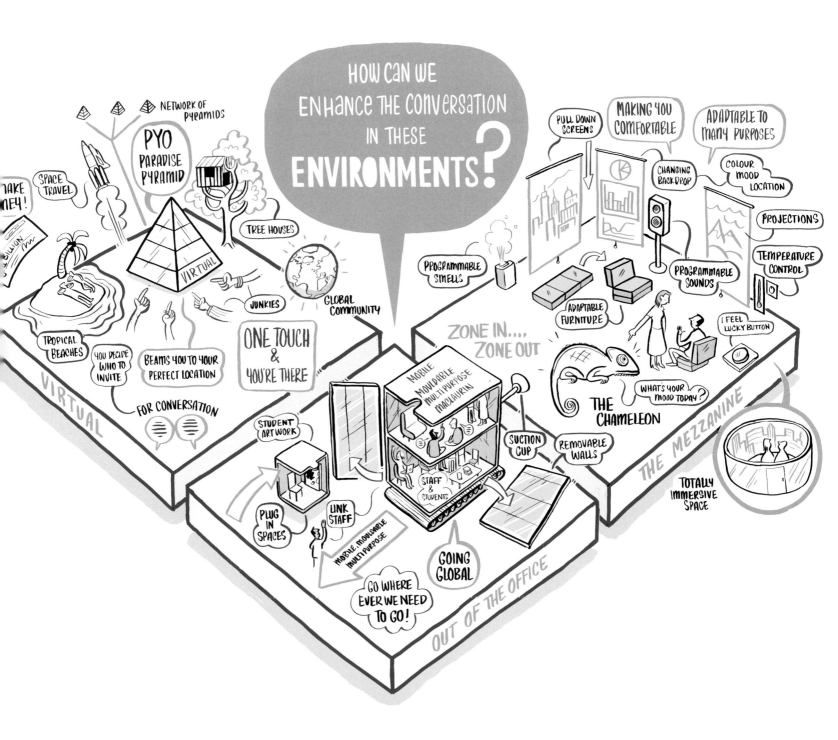

Anna Penkner
Renate Pommerening

designdoppel.de

Topics that are hard to grasp are the most interesting subject matter for visualizations. For the Globale Schnäppchenjagd, images were created digitally on a drawing tablet by Designdoppel aka Anna Penkner and Renate Pommerening. Because the two planned to work together on one drawing, visual consistency was a concern, as was keeping up with the international speakers that would have simultaneous translations between English and German. Knowing this, and that the event would require a high level of concentration over the course of several hours, they needed a system that would allow them to take turns drawing and focusing on the input. Predetermined style and color conventions gave the image visual consistency and it allowed the pair flexibility in taking drawing turns without anyone noticing a difference in style. They also planned the sea life theme ahead of time as a way of making the talk more tangible and as a source of inspiration for the pictures in the detailed areas. Large colored sections served as thematic dividers, while the speakers appear next to each other inside little boats with their core statements underneath them in the blue sea. This structure allows the image to be both easily scanned for detailed content and viewed as a larger landscape.

—

GLOBALE SCHNÄPPCHENJAGD
fig. 1

Client: anonymous
Produced in: Hamburg, Germany, 2016
Technique: Digital
Format: Keynote and discussion
Dimensions: 3840 x 2389px
Time: 4–5 hours

fig. 1

fig. 2

92

GRAPHIC RECORDING BY designdoppel

DESIGNDOPPEL

It's not often that graphic recorders aren't physically present for the talks they record, but that's exactly what happened for Kunden service 4.0. With the use of Skype, Anna Penkner and Renate Pommerening recorded the workshop remotely from their office. Although the time pressure and live drawing aspects of the recording were the same as they would be in person, they found it challenging to be deprived of seeing the audience and their reactions to the drawing in person. During the recording process, their biggest wish was for a smooth Internet connection, because it allowed them to hear the content and transmit the final image, which was then made into a large-format print to decorate the participants' office and motivate them to pursue the changes proposed in the workshop. To minimize complications during the sessions they planned a number of things in advance with the client, including the main concept. The idea was to create a landscape with diverse areas that represented the different values chosen as most important by the participants. Various motifs, including an eagle and a lighthouse, were integrated into the scenery and used for inspiration to develop the different landscape zones.

—

KUNDENSERVICE 4.0
fig. 2

Client: anonymous
Produced in: Hamburg, Germany, 2016
Technique: Digital
Format: Workshop
Dimensions: 0.84 x 1.19 m
Time: 6 hours

DRAWING OUT IDEAS

—

Tanya Gadsby

—

drawingoutideas.ca

—

An interactive graphic recording was the perfect fit for a social networking event hosted by Pretio Interactive. After consulting with the client, graphic recorder Tanya Gadsby planned a playful and energetic recording that involved asking the 150 attendees to take polaroid self-portraits and then connect their portrait with colored ribbon to different parts of the tech landscape of Victoria, BC. In preparation, she designed the title as well as unique visuals to represent each company or technology area. Easily identifiable icons were especially important because the event was fast-paced with multiple people trying to connect themselves to the tech landscape at the same time. It was also critical that the graphic recording feel authentic to the client and participants, so that they would be drawn to engage with it. Strong, bold color and line use also ensured that the visuals popped from underneath the ribbons and their cheeky humor helped to generate a mood of excitement about the graphic recording. The title, which was cut out of foam core and attached to the top of the wall, completed the final piece that stood at ten feet tall and dominated the room.

—

SPRING INTO STARTUP
fig. 1

Client: Pretio Interactive
Produced in: Victoria, Canada, 2015
Technique: Analog
Format: Workshop
Dimensions: 1.2 x 3 m
Time: 2.5 hours

—

IMPACT OF OCEAN RESEARCH
fig. 2

Client: MEOPAR - Marine Environmental Observation Prediction & Response
Produced in: Vancouver, Canada, 2015
Technique: Analog
Format: Workshop
Dimensions: 1.2 x 2.2 m
Time: 1 hour

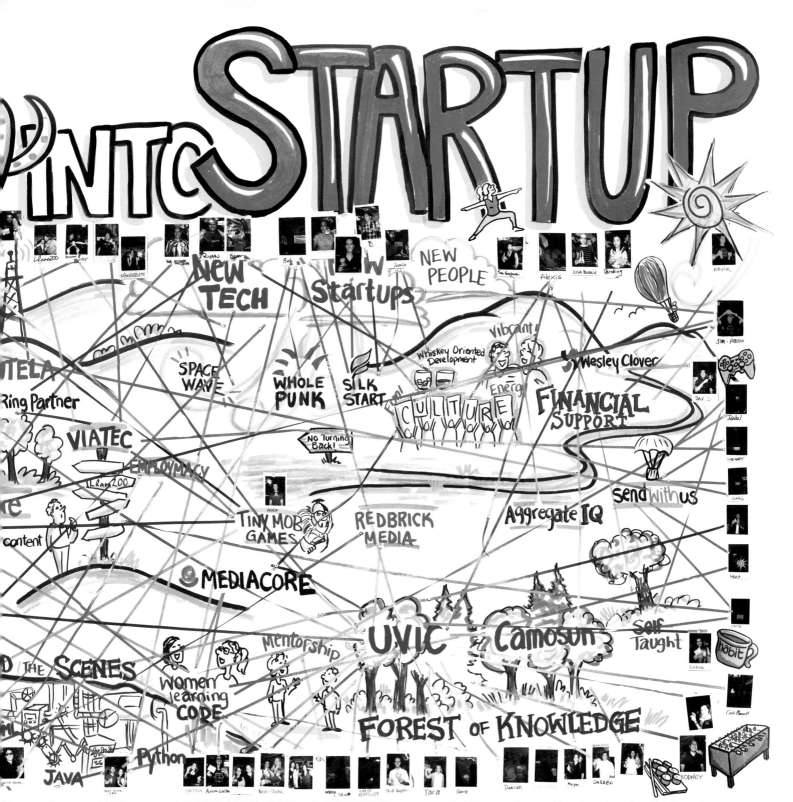

fig. 1

fig. 2

DRAWING OUT IDEAS

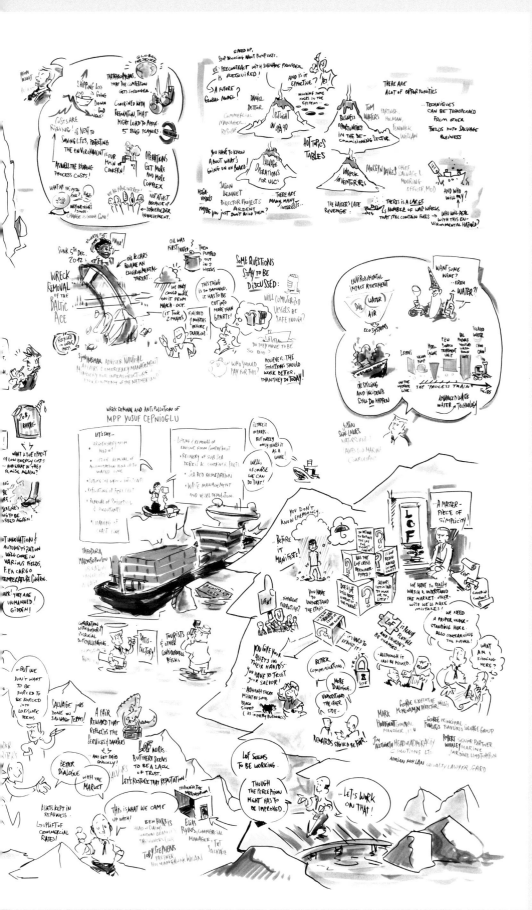

fig. 1

VISUAL FACILITATORS
—
Malte von Tiesenhausen
—
visualfacilitators.com
—

The marine salvage and wreck removal industry is a highly complex and internationally connected field. The annual Salvage and Wreck Conference, held in London, has an almost twenty-year tradition but it wasn't until 2015 that it included graphic recording to enrich its many messages and insights. The conference, which features a wide variety of topics spread out across multi-day summits, can be overwhelming to comprehend. To give it a recognizable structure, Malte von Tiesenhausen sought a structure that could easily differentiate the various events that took the form of either case studies, keynotes, or panel discussions. Although von Tiesenhausen and his team typically do significant preparation before any event, he tries to keep it simple and basic. Intuition is the best guide for him and leads to the best results when used in combination with a loose cartoon style that can be strategically colored for consistency and structure. Many of the team presentations were practical case studies, such as the six shipwrecks, which explicitly showed the various situations in which the unlucky ships found themselves. This included a harbormaster in Bremen who made a controversial decision to give asylum to the occupants of a burning vessel transporting hazardous goods. After the event, the graphic recording was auctioned for charity.

—

SALVAGE AND WRECK CONFERENCE
fig. 1

Client: Informa
Produced in: London, United Kingdom, 2015
Technique: Analog
Format: Conference
Dimensions: 1.5 x 4.5 m
Time: 12 hours

VISUAL FACILITATORS

—

Malte von Tiesenhausen
Mathias Weitbrecht

—

visualfacilitators.com

—

Whenever two graphic recorders work together, the process and final product are a co-creation from beginning to end. Working together can be a challenge, but graphic recording team Visual Facilitators aka Mathias Weitbrecht and Malte von Tiesenhausen have found a way to streamline the process and produce successful recordings. They start by assigning roles that will complement one another, which is the key to delivering a final product that is more

substantial than what either could produce alone. The roles they choose include assigning one person to record information and the other to produce visuals and the connecting background artwork. In addition to providing a detailed account of the event, this process also guarantees a consistent look and feel for the final piece. For the one-day workshop at the Master of Future Administration event in Berlin, their biggest challenge was processing the enormous

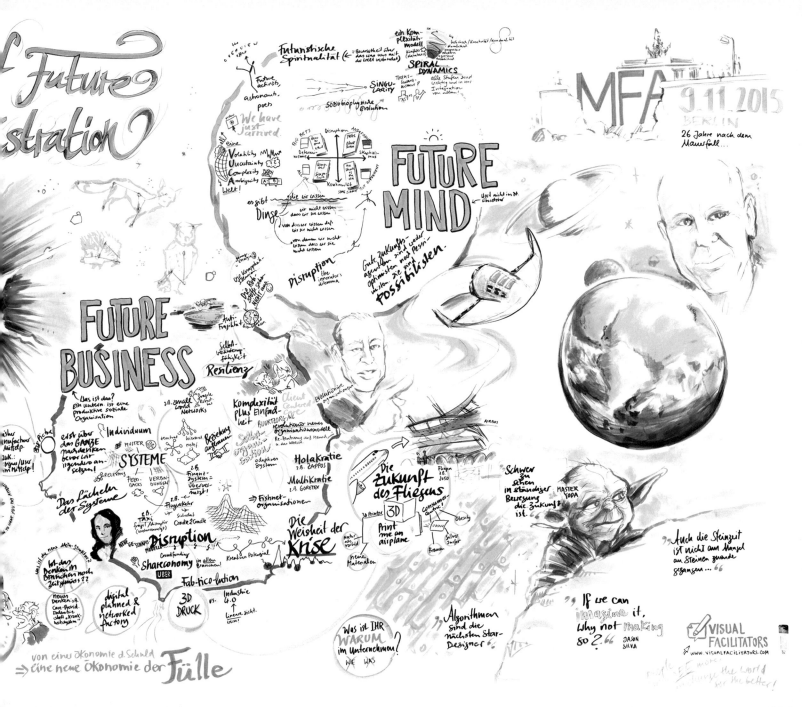

fig. 1

amount of information shared during the content-rich day. Post-It notes became a go-to method for capturing all of the information because they could post them as reminders to each other. In addition, intuition and synchronicity is an important part of the team's ability to manifest a beautiful and wordless workflow.

—

MASTER OF FUTURE ADMINISTRATION WORKSHOP WITH FUTURIST MATTHIAS HORX
fig. 1

Client: Euroforum
Produced in: Berlin, Germany, 2015
Technique: Analog
Format: Workshop
Dimensions: 1.5 x 4.5 m
Time: 7 hours

GRAPHIC FOOTPRINTS

—

Sophia Liang

—

graphicfootprints.com

—

In 2015, Sophia Liang used graphic recording to help ten school districts around the United States clarify and visualize their learning goals at the Graphic Footprints Visioning Workshops. Hosted by Education Elements and the Lexington Institute, each session clarified what the teams wanted to achieve together and what they needed to tackle moving forward. At the end of the process, the ten maps showcased in the final workshop showed connections between the diverse conversations.

In preparation, Liang and the facilitator designed an agenda based on research about each school district. At the end of the session, one cohesive vision map was created through conversations structured to answer three questions: What does your vision look like? Why does it matter? What are your next steps and priorities?

Through active listening, Liang decided what was written and drawn on the map, how it was structured, and how the sections should connect to one another. Working in a cartoon style with bright colors, the map became a communication tool for students and parents, reflecting the personality of each school and team.

—

**PERSONALIZED LEARNING -
VISIONING SESSIONS**
fig. 1

Client: Education Elements, Lexington Institute
Produced in: Various cities, 2015
Technique: Analog
Format: Workshop
Dimensions: 1.2 x 2.4 m
Time: 4 hours

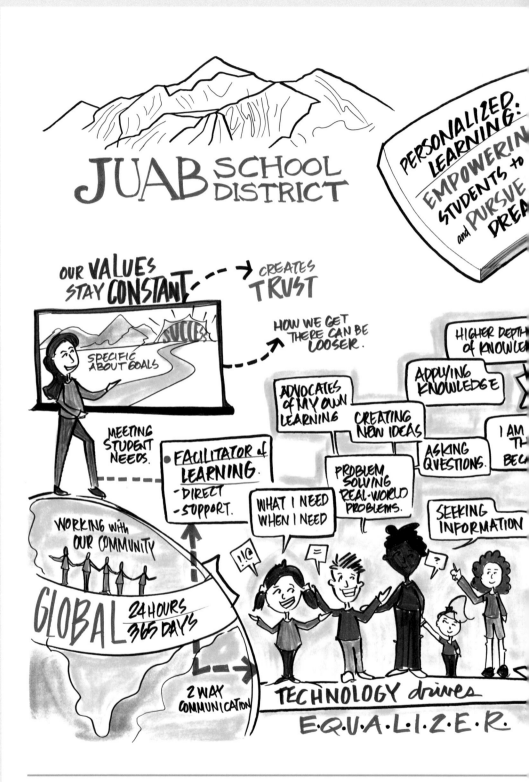

fig. 1

fig. 2

GRAPHIC HARVEST

—

Sonja Niederhumer

—

graphicharvest.co.za

—

fig. 1

During the Deloitte Investing in African Mining Indaba event, participants shared their opinions on the future of mining in Africa. Graphic recorder Sonja Niederhumer visualized the event workshops on the wall, capturing key ideas for creating social change through design. The process of the recording was completely collaborative, with each image based on conversations between Niederhumer and attendees.

After sharing and visualizing what they felt was most important, the group decided which image best represented their ideas as a whole. The result is an exciting conversation map outlining three days of collaboration, ideas, and sharing.

Using the Deloitte brand colors, Niederhumer worked with markers on a white board, always asking the person she was speaking with what their specific idea looked like. In this way, they made the images their own and she was just a visual translator. Though the unusual technique is not visible in the final piece, it was effective and the content it produced was a standout feature of the recording.

—

DELOITTE MINING INDABA
fig. 1–2

Client: Deloitte South Africa
Produced in: Cape Town, South Africa, 2016
Technique: Analog
Format: Conference
Dimensions: 2 x 3 m
Time: 36 hours

GRAPHIC HARVEST

–

Grant Johnson
Sonja Niederhumer

–

graphicharvest.co.za

–

The visual recording for Abalobi Fishers Journey tells the story of the struggles and challenges of local fishermen while simultaneously giving a deep sense of how interconnected we all are. It also illustrates real evidence of climate change as experienced by the fishermen and how they work with the Abalobi team to improve the Abalobi app as well as their livelihoods. Based on the four main questions of the World Cafe Workshop, the structure of the recording and the visuals themselves came from listening to participants to discover what their boats and fish species look like. The team also walked around the harbor before the workshop to take reference photos of the different boats. The recording shows the story building from time spent at sea, going to the marketplace, and how they connect to governmental policies. Because most of the participants spoke Afrikaans, there was a small language barrier but it was overcome by checking in with

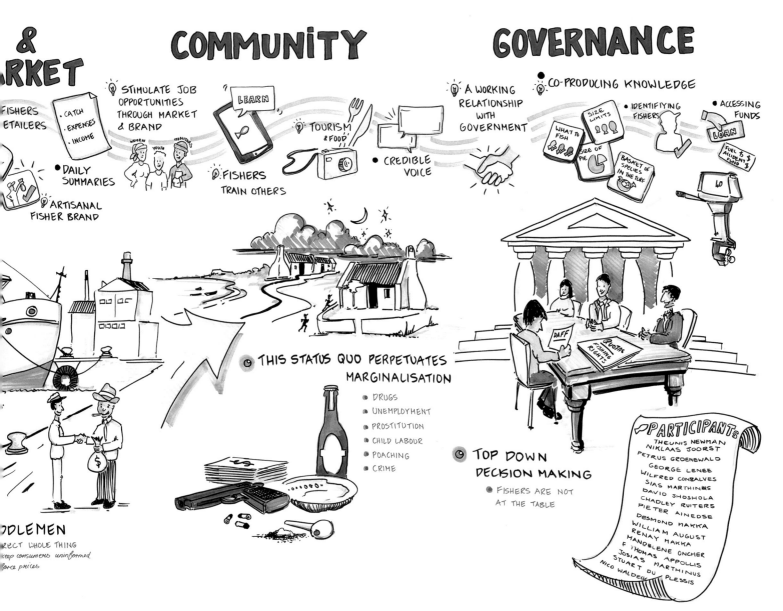

...IERS JOURNEY

...ARKET
COMMUNITY
GOVERNANCE

- FISHERS
  ...ETAILERS
  - CATCH
  - EXPENSES
  - INCOME
- DAILY SUMMARIES
- ARTISANAL FISHER BRAND

- STIMULATE JOB OPPORTUNITIES THROUGH MARKET & BRAND
  (WOMEN, YOUTH, MONITORS)

- LEARN
- TOURISM & FOOD
- FISHERS TRAIN OTHERS

- A WORKING RELATIONSHIP WITH GOVERNMENT
- CREDIBLE VOICE

- CO-PRODUCING KNOWLEDGE
  - WHAT TO FISH
  - SIZE LIMITS
  - SIZE OF PIE
  - BASKET OF SPECIES IN THE TURF
- IDENTIFYING FISHERS
- ACCESSING FUNDS
  - LOAN
  - FUEL & ALLIANCE FUND

- THIS STATUS QUO PERPETUATES MARGINALISATION
  - DRUGS
  - UNEMPLOYMENT
  - PROSTITUTION
  - CHILD LABOUR
  - POACHING
  - CRIME

- TOP DOWN DECISION MAKING
  - FISHERS ARE NOT AT THE TABLE

DAFF

QUOTA FISHING RIGHTS

PARTICIPANTS
THEUNIS NEWMAN
NIKLAAS JOORST
PETRUS GROENEWALD
GEORGE LENEE
WILFRED GONZALVES
SIAS MARTHINUS
DAVID SHOSHOLA
CHADLEY RUITERS
PIETER AINEDSE
DESMOND MAKKA
WILLIAM AUGUST
RENAY MAKKA
MANDELENE ONCHER
F THOMAS APPOLLIS
JOSIAS MARTHINUS
STUART DU PLESSIS
NICO WALDEW

...DDLEMEN
...RECT WHOLE THING
...eep consumers uninformed
...force prices

fig. 1

people after a discussion or quickly checking on Google to make sure details were accurate. Ultimately the decision was made to do the graphic in four parts based on the four World Cafe questions and to show information related to the Abalobi app in a flow line on the top.

—

ABALOBI FISHERS JOURNEY
fig. 1–2

Client: Abalobi and University of Cape Town
Produced in: Cape Town, South Africa, 2015
Technique: Analog
Format: Workshop
Dimensions: 1 x 2.5 m
Time: 8 hours

fig. 2

GABRIELE HEINZEL

—

gabriele-heinzel.com

—

Parallel workshops are not always a graphic recorder's favorite challenge—it's easy to miss information in them, and when groups only have a few minutes to present their results to the audience, the graphic recorder has to draw extra quickly. This was the exact setup for the DB Schenker conference in Potsdam, where Gabriele Heinzel recorded multiple workshops.

Managing to record short insights during the workshops, which she prepared during the breaks before the presentations, she then bound them together on a large roll of paper. The recording became a mixture of talks and Q&As represented on the left side of the image with the results of the five workshop sessions placed to the right. Starting with the headline picture on the top left, she drew on logistics imagery—ships, trains, containers, and a plane—all of which reappear in other images. Splitting the recording in two made sense because it echoed the structure of the event. Feeling that a graphic recording should organize the content and show the connections between talks, Heinzel relies heavily on visual connecting elements that allow her to be playful or ironic and set visual anchors to help viewers navigate the information later on.

—

CONFERENCE WITH WORKSHOP SESSIONS FOR DB SCHENKER
fig. 1

Client: DB Schenker
Produced in: Potsdam, Germany, 2014
Technique: Analog
Format: Keynote and Workshop
Dimensions: 1.4 × 0.7 m
Time: 1 day

—

STARTUP CONFERENCE ACCELERATE@HHL
fig. 2

Client: HHL Leipzig Graduate School of Management
Produced in: Leipzig, Germany, 2015
Technique: Analog
Format: Keynote
Dimensions: 1.25 × 3 m
Time: 1 day

fig. 1

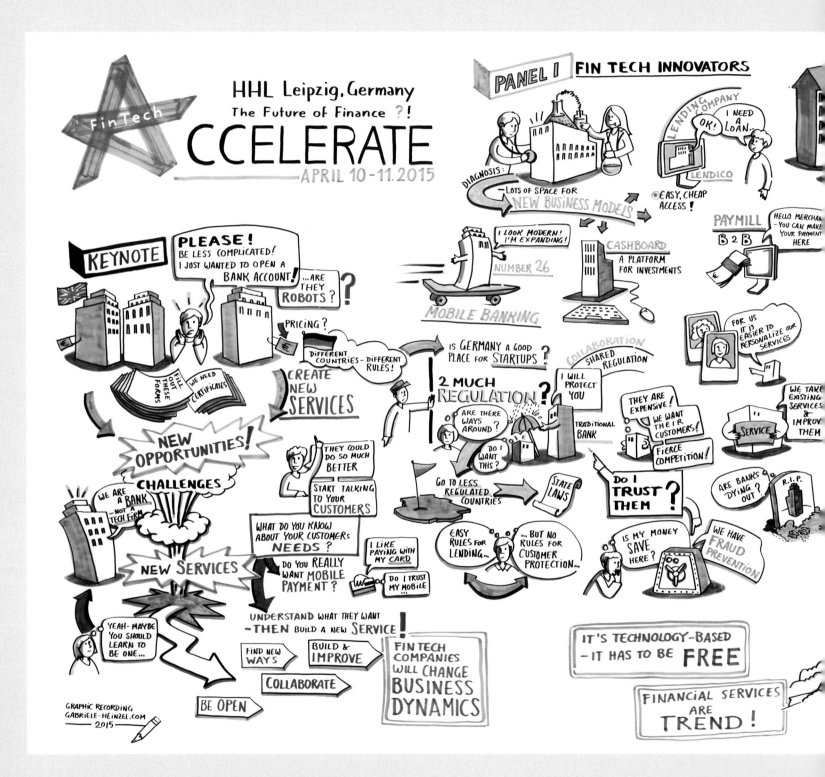

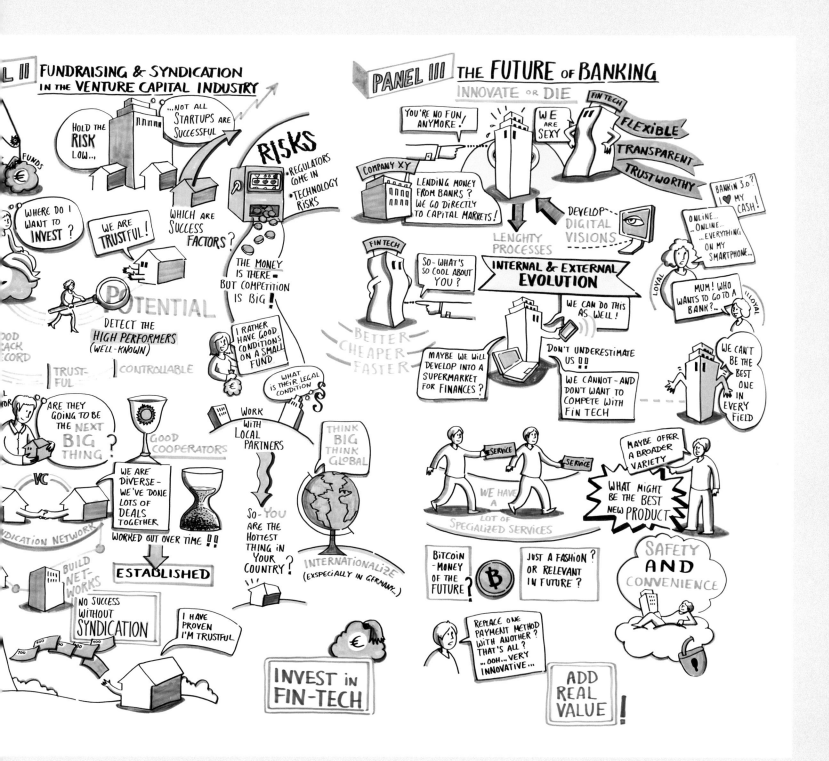

GABRIELE HEINZEL

fig. 2

fig. 1

fig. 2

GABRIELE HEINZEL

—

gabriele-heinzel.com

—

For the conference Energiewende im Kopf held in Witten, Germany, graphic recorder Gabriele Heinzel sat in on workshops and keynote sessions devoted to why energy transition is so hard for individuals to embrace. Because the event took place over the course of two days and included a variety of formats including keynote speeches, discussions, and round tables, the client decided to build a special wall for the recording. Although Heinzel doesn't consider herself a short person, the format was so large that she had to use a ladder to reach the top.

To give the large image some structure, she stuck to shades of orange and green, which also helped set the speeches and different formats apart from one another. This technique makes them easy to identify and also allowed them to stand on their own. The single speeches, which are placed on the left side, can easily speak for themselves while the content on the right includes the more interactive events like workshops and discussions. Heinzel found that the wall did its job during the session breaks; participants could regularly be found gathered in front of it, going over the information and discussing it with others.

—

2 DAY CONFERENCE ON
"ENERGIEWENDE IM KOPF"
fig. 1–2

Client: Energieagentur NRW
Produced in: Witten, Germany, 2014
Technique: Analog
Format: Keynotes, workshops and discussions
Dimensions: 2.5 x 4 m
Time: 2 days

HOUSATONIC

—

Alfredo Carlo
Marcello Petruzzi

—

housatonic.eu

—

fig. 1

In preparation for the graphic recording at the Bluesign Conference in St. Gallen, Switzerland, Alfredo Carlo and Marcello Petruzzi decided to do very little advance planning to capture the two-day conference in one large, content-rich image. Other than incorporating the conference's branding into a blue sign along the wall, which Carlo and Petruzzi drew before the event started, they waited to start work until they were on site. Once the conference started, they took inspiration and direction from the speakers, listening to and translating their words in the moment.

Ultimately, it was the small work area that proved to be the most challenging part of the recording. In the end, there was just enough space for the collected content, which flows through one continuous image, creating a path for the audience to follow.

Varying proportions and color-coding helped organize and structure information; blue and yellow were the prominent colors with enlarged key words written in red.

Their choice of materials included erasable markers, which allowed the team freedom and flexibility to play with positive and negative space.

—

BLUESIGN CONFERENCE
fig. 1

Client: Bluesign
Produced in: St. Gallen, Switzerland, 2015
Technique: Analog
Format: Conference
Dimensions: 12 × 2 m
Time: 24 hours

fig. 1
Alfredo Carlo's thoughts on Housatonic's graphic recording with Marcello Petruzzi for the Bluesign Conference.

—

114

July 13/14, 2015, St. Gallen, Switzerland DO, D

Detail zoom

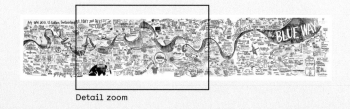

Detail zoom

116

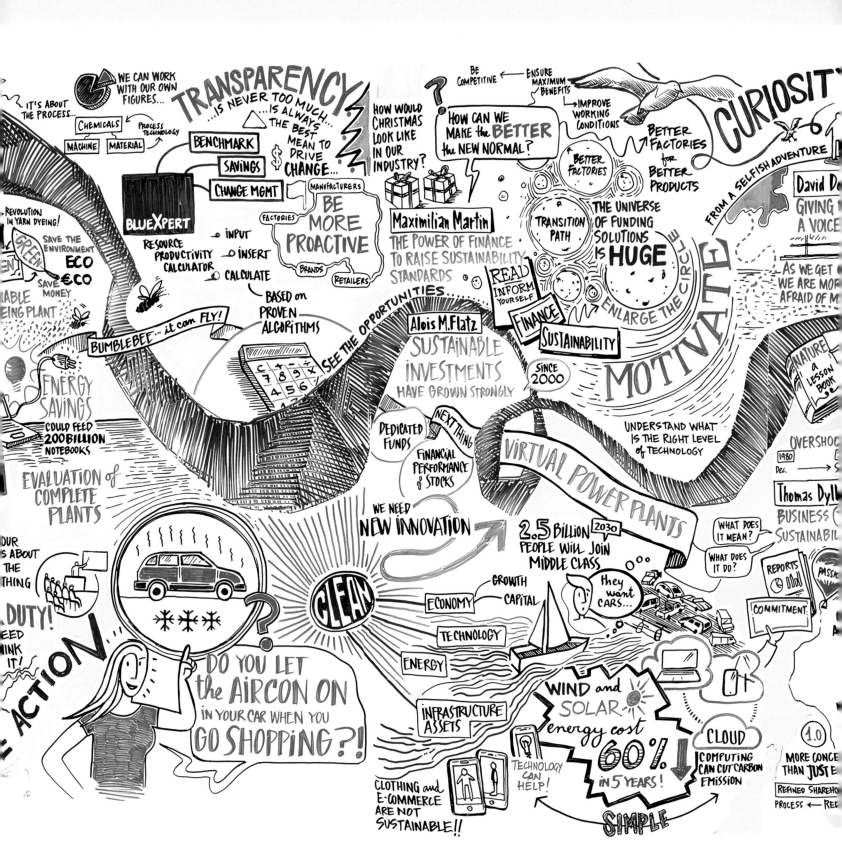

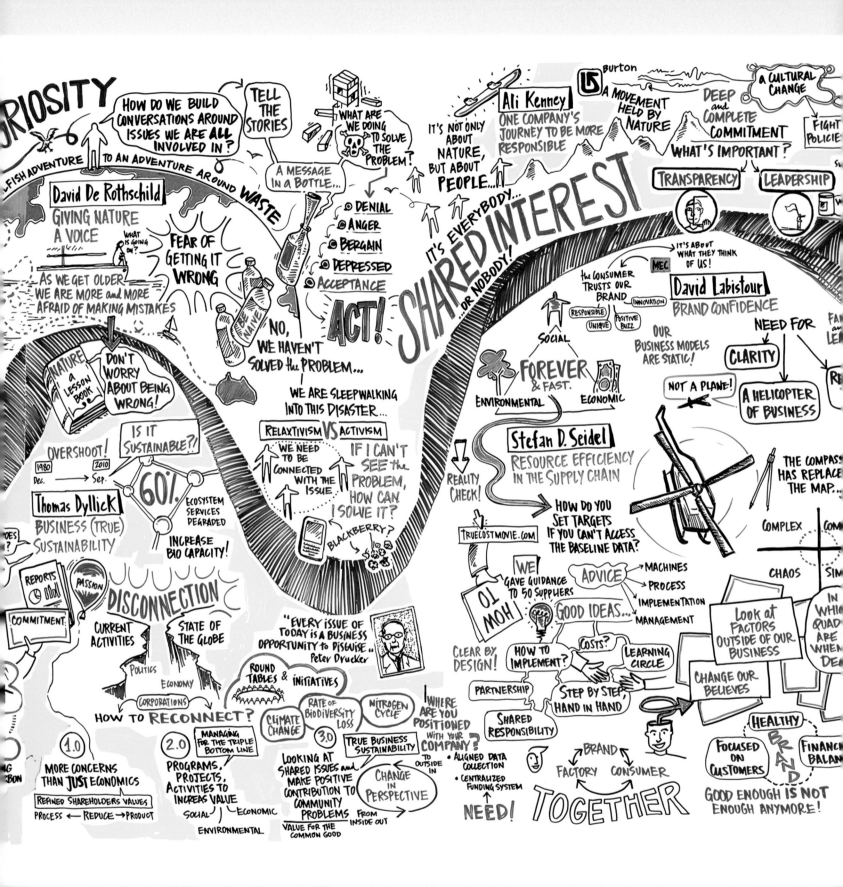

Detail zoom

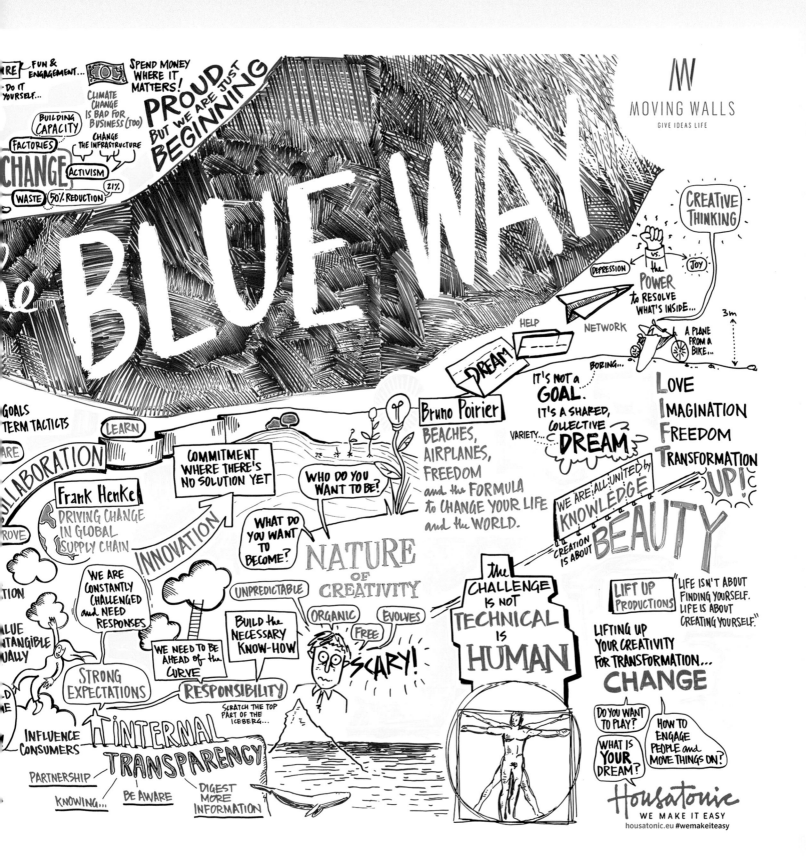

HOUSATONIC

—

Alfredo Carlo

—

housatonic.eu

—

Alfredo Carlo of Housatonic worked for the three days on the knowledge wall for the International Baccalaureate Organization's conference in Macau, China. The 12×12 meter wall summarized the various sessions and presentations for participants, giving them an overview of all the sessions—even the ones they didn't have a chance to participate in. The graphic layout and the metaphor are based on the conference theme, which centered on how education influences the future. Carlo used large graffiti markers to fill in large surfaces and a mix of key words and small details to fill in the spaces. The words help people recognize and identify what they are looking for, while the drawings help visualize the information. Housatonic colleague Jodi worked alongside Carlo to help provide content from the different conference rooms. Ultimately the visuals combined the conference imagery with Carlo's intuitive drawings, creating a final piece that connects the images with what the sessions were talking about.

—

IBO KNOWLEDGE WALL
fig. 1

Client: International Baccalaureate Organization
Produced in: Macau, China, 2015
Technique: Analog
Format: Conference
Dimensions: 12 × 2 m
Time: 36 hours

fig. 1

Detail zoom

Detail zoom

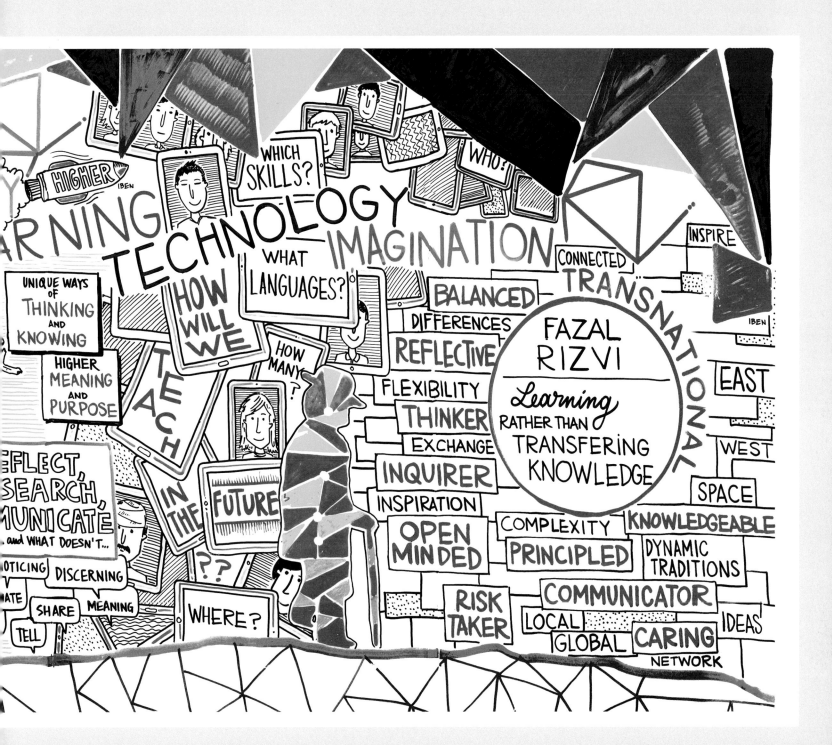

THE VALUE WEB

—

Alfredo Carlo
Christoph J Kellner

—

thevalueweb.org

—

Detail zoom

Over the course of a busy three-day conference, participants often miss certain pieces of information or want a souvenir of what they learned and experienced. The Lego Foundation Knowledge Wall, created by graphic recorders Alfredo Carlo and Christoph J. Kellner, gave participants a reference point for all of the topics covered as well as a tangible way to photograph and share what they'd learned at the conference.

The two decided on a visually dynamic plan that used textural mixed media to create large and small elements in juxtaposition with one another. They also developed a set of characters to deliver the messages, with different lettering styles to give voice to them and highlight key messages. With a centrally located position in the conference area, the team worked on a large S-shaped wall that gave participants a good view of the recording as it evolved. During the creation phase, the audience was encouraged to contribute with comments. It was fun to react to their input even though it was a challenge to ensure that everyone's voice was heard.

Building off of large letters drawn as the background, Carlo and Kellner created a dynamic visual interaction between colors, images, and letters. The result was a recording that can be enjoyed as a whole or in smaller details that tell the story of the three-day conference.

—

LEGO FOUNDATION KNOWLEDGE WALL
fig. 1

Client: Lego Foundation
Produced in: Billund, Denmark, 2015
Technique: Analog
Format: Conference
Dimensions: 8 × 3 m
Time: 30 hours

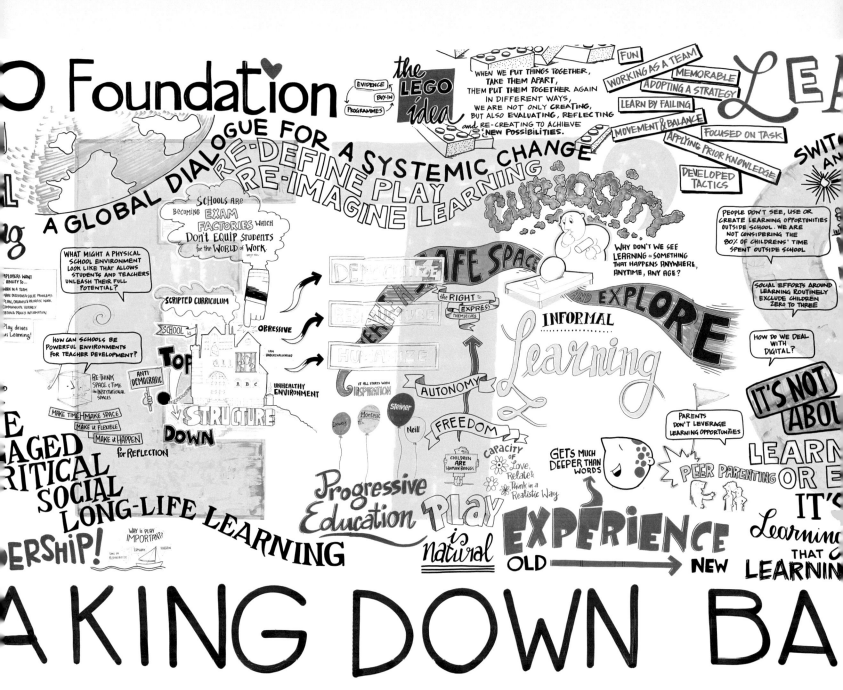

fig. 1

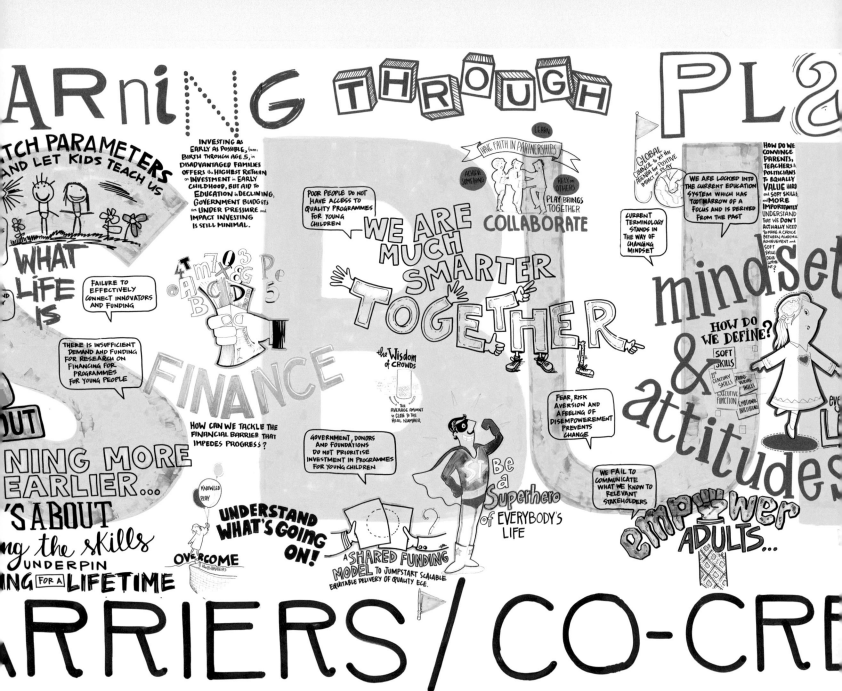

BREAKING DOWN BARRIERS / CO-CREATING SOLUTIONS
THE LEGO
IDEA CONFERENCE 2015

Detail zoom

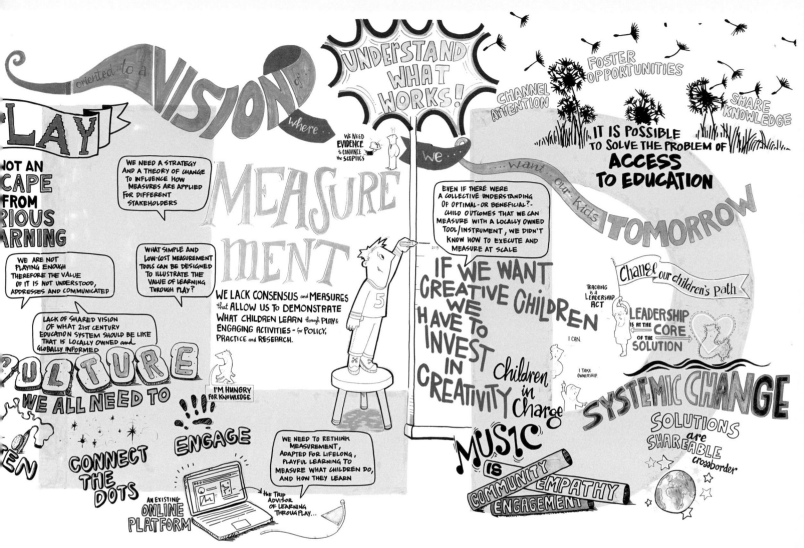

ZUPPASSION

—

Alessandro Bonaccorsi

—

zuppassion.com

—

fig. 1

The combination of listening and watching is a powerful tool for helping people remember experiences and information—and it's the reason graphic recording continues to grow in popularity for workshops and events. Looking for higher engagement from its party members, the Democratic Party of Bologna developed a facilitation process and looked to graphic recorder Alessandro Bonaccorsi to help demonstrate how it works. Bonaccorsi, who believes concepts are easily forgotten unless they are paired with experience, always projects his drawings onto the wall so that the audience can see the images come alive through shape, color, and lettering. In doing so, he finds that his audience engages in the process and absorbs the concepts of the talks more deeply. With a background in illustration, Bonaccorsi prefers conceptual images to clichés or cartoons because they represent new ways of thinking about ideas. His work transforms the graphic recording into a map of signs, symbols, and glyphs that ideally becomes a document that can be understood by anyone, even when taken out of context. The success of his approach is also based on an openness to the speakers he works with, and a spontaneous response to their message that reveals the essence of its content.

—

**DEMOCRATIC PARTY BOLOGNA:
FACILITATION PROCESS**
fig. 1–4

Client: Democratic Party Bologna
Produced in: Bologna, Italy, 2014
Technique: Digital
Format: Workshop
Dimensions: 0.7 x 1 m
Time: 12 hours

fig. 2

fig. 3

fig. 4

INK FACTORY

—

inkfactorystudio.com

—

Originally conceived as a panel discussion on innovative ways to leverage the landscape around Chicago, Architecture from the Skyscraper to the Riverwalk pivoted midway through the session and became a broader discussion on how architecture can enhance quality of life for people in any location. This unexpected change of course required graphic recorders Ink Factory to be flexible on a number of issues. Visually they had to bring the conversation back to the heart of the discussion while still using the architectural elements they had planned in advance. The pre-drawn title went unchanged, as did the recording's colors, which were based on the Chicago flag. These graphics and color systems highlighted main points and key themes. Blue represented the key talking points from the panel discussion, while pictograms and glyphs reinforced the overall theme.

In addition to the abrupt change in format and subject matter, the physical location for the graphic recording became a challenge of its own: positioned at the top of the auditorium in a small, cramped space surrounded by people walking in and out of the auditorium, the team had to adjust to working and listening in difficult conditions.

fig. 1

ARCHITECTURE
fig. 1

Client: Chicago Ideas Week
Produced in: Chicago, IL, USA, 2015
Technique: Analog
Format: Conference
Dimensions: 1.1 x 1.7 m
Time: 1.5 hours

—

URBAN INNOVATION
fig. 2–3

Client: Chicago Ideas Week
Produced in: Chicago, IL, USA, 2015
Technique: Analog
Format: Conference
Dimensions: 1.1 x 1.7 m
Time: 75 minutes

fig. 2

fig. 3

MARIE JACOBI

—

visualrecording.de

—

fig. 1

The graphic recording by Marie Jacobi for DB Regio AG & S-Bahn München was created interactively with the participants during the company's open house day. The participants were young adults who spoke with Jacobi about their ideas surrounding the eight themes of the day. She then listened and translated the ideas in real time. Her particular choice of only two colors plus one primary color—black colored in red and green with some blue—divided the image into two areas. On the left side is Munich's S-Bahn and on the right side is Deutsche Bahn with each area containing four topics. To make the separation between topics clearly visible, she made a clear cut by the title of white characters on a black background. The biggest challenge of the project was working with participants all around her as they came and went and spoke to her directly. The recording was done interactively. Ultimately 95% of the graphic recording was improvised in real time with the remaining 5% planned ahead of time including the logos, style of the title, and the color choice.

—

WAS BEWEGT UNS MORGEN?
(WHAT WILL MOVE US TOMORROW?)
fig. 1–2

Client: DB Regio AG & S-Bahn München
Produced in: Germany, 2014
Technique: Analog
Format: Workshop
Dimensions: 1.4 x 2 m
Time: 5–6 hours

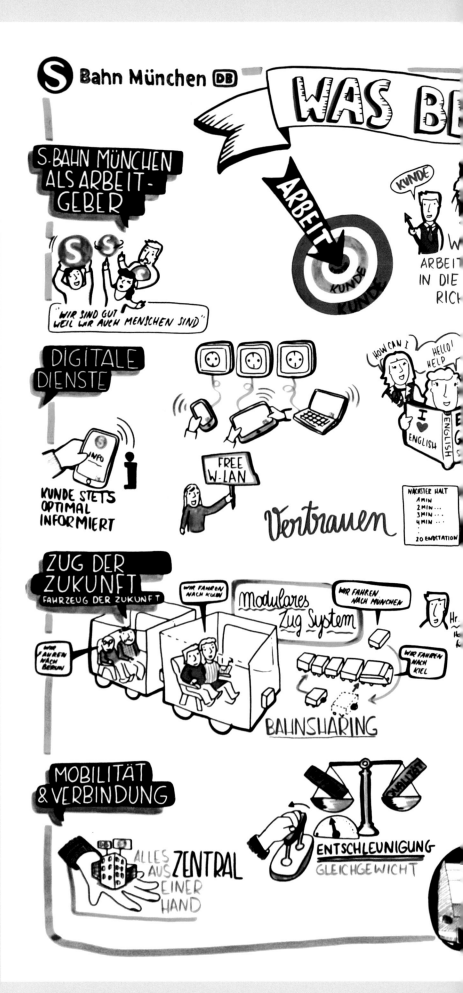

fig. 2

JONGENS VAN DE TEKENINGEN

—

Piet van Rosmalen
Willem Minderhoud

—

jongensvandetekeningen.nl

—

Force11 asked Jongens van de Tekeningen to create a live visual summary of their conference on research communication and e-scholarship at Oxford in 2015. During the two-day event, van de Tekeningen and his team used pencils, Neuland markers, and white Molotov markers to fill a 4.5 × 2 meter sheet of paper with highlights of the event. Knowing they wanted to create something that delivered a substantial visual impact, they combined the size of the wall with bold color choices to attract attention. Working from a philosophy that graphic recorders need to be concrete and simple in how they communicate, they used a blue background that worked well in contrast with white as the highlight color. This made the elements pop, especially next to the large black surfaces, and because this was a conference on science communication, the choice helped participants make a connection to their own work. A general plan to create islands for each of the speakers was the only decision made ahead of time; the rest was devised on the spot with the help of ladders to reach the highest parts of the wall. Over the course of the conference, the wall fulfilled van de Tekeningen's wish that it become a focal point by becoming not only a record of the event, but also a meeting place for speakers and attendees where they could connect and share information.

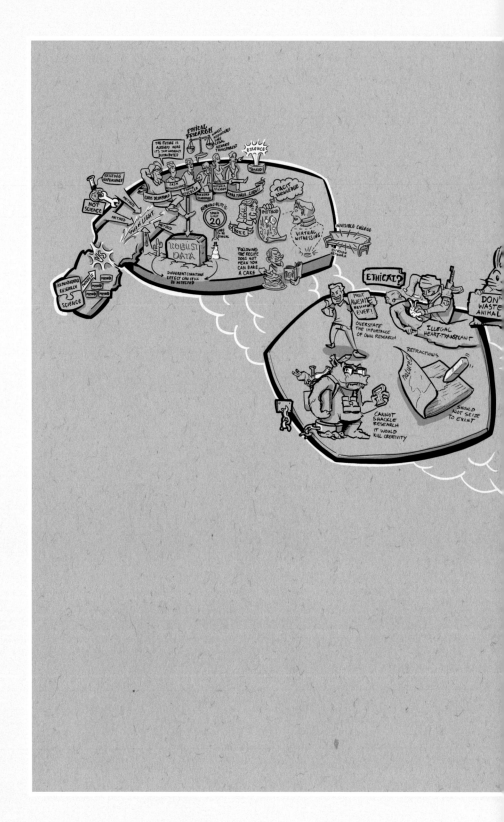

—

VISUAL RECORDING AT FORCE 2015
fig. 1

Client: Force11
Produced in: Oxford, United Kingdom, 2015
Technique: Analog
Format: Keynote
Dimensions: 4.5 × 2 m
Time: 2 days

fig. 1

Detail zoom

Detail zoom

JONGENS VAN DE TEKENINGEN

—

**Willem Minderhoud
Robert Smit
Piet van Rosmalen
Tomas Pasma**

—

jongensvandetekeningen.nl

—

Technology Foundation STW helps transfer knowledge between the technical sciences and users. During their annual conference in Utrecht, graphic recorder Jongens van de Tekeningen and his team visualized the pitches scientists made to a panel of experts and the discussions that followed them. Using Neuland markers, the scribes drew each theme on a large sheet of paper mounted onto foam core panels. These drawings were then distributed throughout the room and placed at the center of group discussions on the related topic. Working with two illustrators, a general style outline was created to help maintain visual consistency and the conference themes were then divided between the illustrators. The drawings were made with just two simple colors that also represented the client's logo: black for outlines and gray for shading. After the conference, all of the pieces were digitized and enhanced in Photoshop.

—

STW CONGRESS
fig. 1–5

Client: STW/Room for IDs
Produced in: Utrecht, Netherlands, 2015
Technique: Analog
Format: Workshop
Dimensions: 0.84 x 1.2 m each
Time: 4 hours

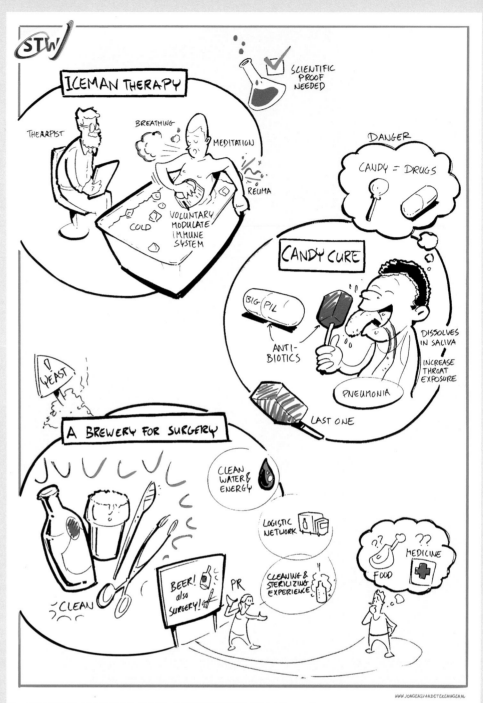

fig. 1

fig. 2

fig. 3

fig. 4

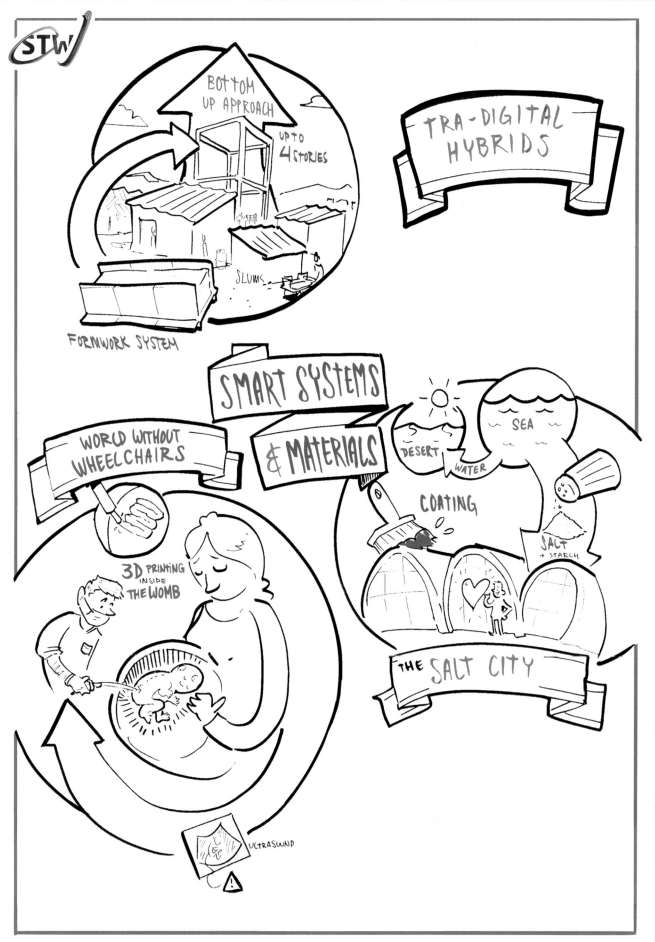

JULIAN KÜCKLICH

—

playability.de

—

Recording the stories of Hiroshima survivors with impact and accuracy for the ICAN Civil Society Forum was a great honor for Julian Kücklich. After thinking about the most effective approach to recording the unimaginable horrors of these experiences, he decided to forgo his usual advance planning and opted instead to make the most of his creative choices in the moment. In doing so, he began the recordings knowing only what his color palette would be—a bold combination of black, gray, and red that connected the talk to the Civil Society Forum's visual identity.

As survivor Setsuko Thurlow's story unfolded on stage, Kücklich found her words to be the most powerful representation of such an incomprehensible event and began to base the structure of the recording around them. The images he did choose to include, such as a woman holding the outline of a missing person, were emotional reactions to her story of the suffering of the Hiroshima survivors.

Kücklich's choice to keep planning before the event to a minimum would not work for every graphic recording, but in this case it was the perfect match for the subject matter. It brought out an intuitive and heartfelt response to a cause whose success is rooted in human connection and empathy.

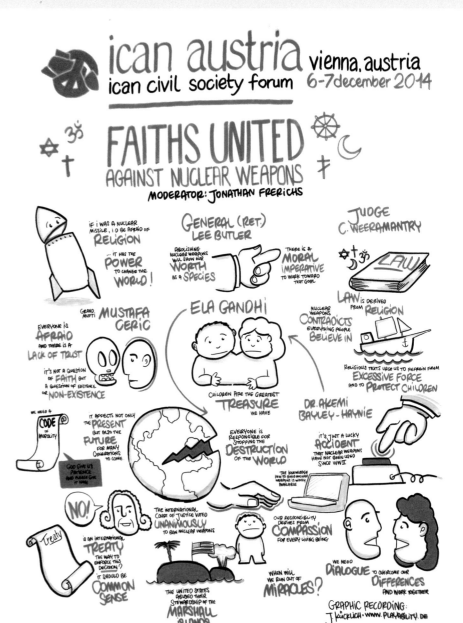

fig. 1

—

CIVIL SOCIETY FORUM
fig. 1–3

Client: ICAN Austria
Produced in: Vienna, Austria, 2014
Technique: Analog
Format: Keynote and conference
Dimensions: 1.4 x 1 m each
Time: 12 hours

—

MEDIA & MAKERS JUBA (SOUTH SUDAN)
fig. 4–5

Client: MICT - Media in Cooperation and Transition
Produced in: Juba, South Sudan, 2012
Technique: Analog
Format: Workshop
Dimensions: 0.3 x 0.4 m each
Time: 16 hours

fig. 2

ican austria
ican civil society forum
vienna, austria 6-7 december 2014

fig. 3

fig. 4

fig. 5

JULIAN KÜCKLICH

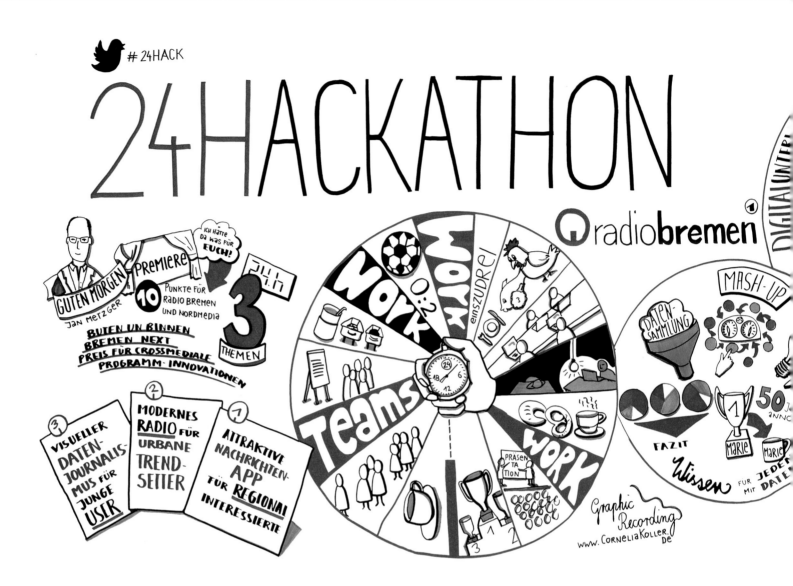

CORNELIA KOLLER

—

corneliakoller.de

—

The only thing graphic recorder Cornelia Koller knew about the 24Hackathon was that they develop apps. Her color choices, based on the Hackathon's red and black logo, create a striking image while the circles represent the closed structure of a hackathon. During the event, participants were split into three groups to develop three different apps. With this in mind, she placed the results and the presentations into circles.

—

24HACKATHON
fig. 1

Client: nordmedia – Film- und Mediengesellschaft Niedersachsen/Bremen mbH, Radio Bremen
Produced in: Bremen, Germany, 2015
Technique: Analog
Format: Hackathon
Dimensions: 1 x 3 m
Time: 24 hours

—

TECHNO EXPO
fig. 2

Client: yellowmonkey Werbeagentur GmbH, TECHNO-EINKAUF GmbH
Produced in: Hamburg, Germany, 2015
Technique: Analog
Format: Exhibition
Dimensions: 1 x 3 m
Time: 8 hours

—

WIE WILLST DU LEBEN?
fig. 3

Client: Communico GmbH
Produced in: Wiesensee, Germany, 2015
Technique: Analog
Format: Keynote
Dimensions: 1 x 2.5 m
Time: 3 hours

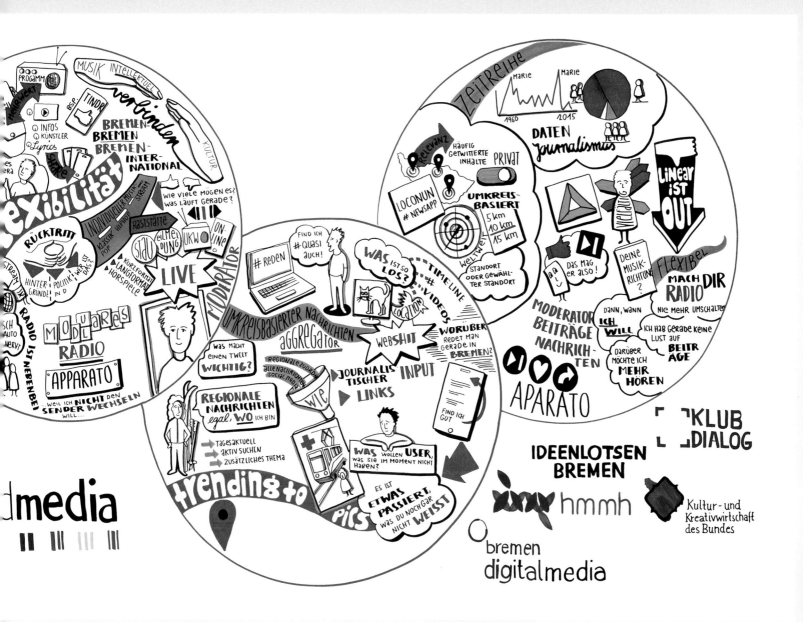

fig. 1

fig. 2

KOMMUNIKATIONS-LOTSEN

—

Andreas Gaertner

—

kommunikationslotsen.de

—

The most striking aspect of Andreas Gaertner's graphic recording for the Telekom Austria Group is its resemblance to a vintage map. This aesthetic decision was influenced by the client's request, prompting Gartner to choose colors and textures that conjure images of a treasure map. For Gaertner, pen and paper is the most interesting and expressive technique for a graphic recording. The process of this work is challenging for him because it involves simultaneously listening,

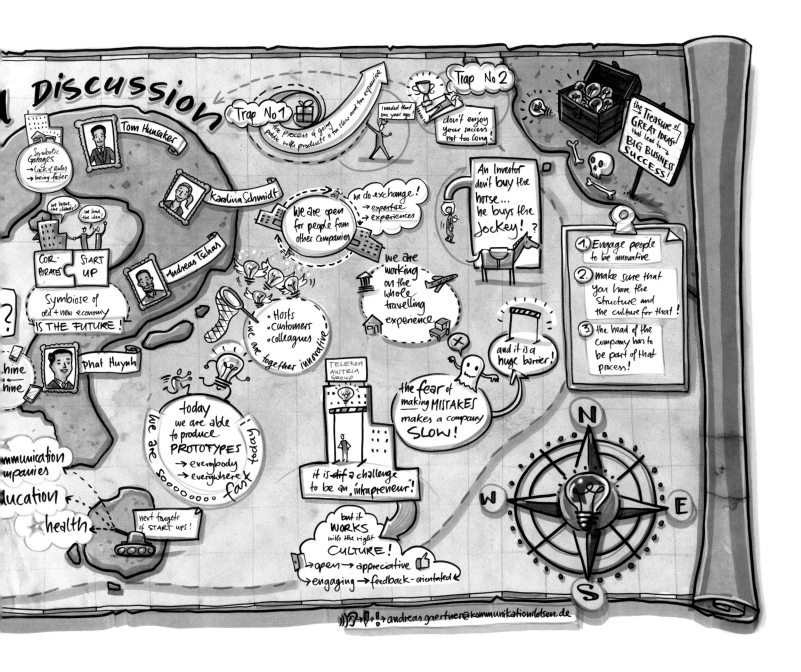

fig. 1

thinking, drawing, and keeping a visual structure in mind. To do this, he practices drawing so often that it becomes automatic, letting him focus on listening and thinking. The only thing Gaertner planned in advance was the map aesthetic and the title.

—

TELEKOM AUSTRIA GROUP / BUSINESS SCHOOL IMPACT
fig. 1

Client: TELEKOM AUSTRIA GROUP
Produced in: Vienna, Austria, 2014
Technique: Analog
Format: Discussion
Dimensions: 1.15 x 3 m
Time: 5 h

ANNE LEHMANN

—

annelehmann.de

—

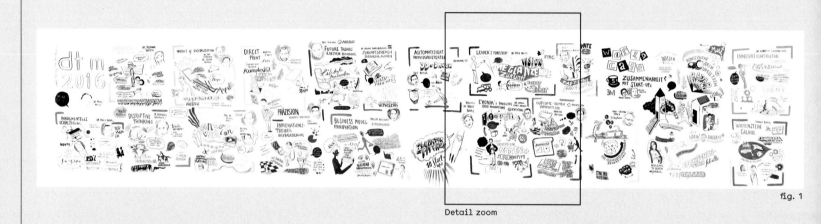

Detail zoom

fig. 1

The speed of the D.TIM conference was breakneck; over the course of two days, Anne Lehmann recorded 20 keynote speeches lasting just 30 minutes apiece. With few breaks in between, the challenge became differentiating between the different speakers and their content, while at the same time developing one cohesive image in which all of the content came together.

As an experienced graphic recorder, Lehmann knew that working on numerous large panels would require emphasizing select details. Since all of the speeches were equally important, it wasn't possible to use size for visual emphasis without implying a ranking of importance. Instead she achieved emphasis by using a color-coding system in combination with varying styles of hand-lettering. Lehmann used other techniques to bring the picture to life as well: contrasts between positive and negative space, color, line work, and the use of cartoon elements.

Despite her seasoned approach, the challenge at this event was keeping up with the pace of the talks, which were dense in specialized information. The solution required removing a few main points from the flood of content and consistently employing core elements like size and typography, portraits of the speakers, and company logos for a unified visual effect.

—

D.TIM CONFERENCE 2016
fig. 1

Client: we.conect
Produced in: Berlin, Germany, 2016
Technique: Analog
Format: Keynotes and conference
Dimensions: 1 x 6 m
Time: 15 hours

—

FRANKFURT BOOK FAIR 2015
fig. 3–4

Client: Frankfurter Buchmesse
Produced in: Frankfurt, Germany, 2015
Technique: Analog
Format: Keynotes
Dimensions: 0.7 x 1 m
Time: 6 hours

fig. 2

fig. 1
Anne Lehmann's graphic recording for the D.TIM Conference in 2016 is an example of the vast amount of information processed and recorded by graphic recorders in a short amount of time.

—

fig. 2
Anne Lehmann drawing live at the Frankfurt Book Fair 2013.

—

HAIDAR BAGIR

VISION

THE MARKETS INDONESIA

THE RAPID PACE OF CHANGE IN INDONESIAN PUBLISHING

GRAPHIC RECORDING
ANNE LEHMANN.DE

154

fig. 3

ROBERT KIM

THE MARKETS SOUTH KOREA

SOUTH KOREA'S EDUCATION MARKET OFFERS DIGITAL AND GLOBAL OPPORTUNITIES

SEBASTIAN LÖRSCHER

—

sebastian-loerscher.de

—

Future smart cities and the relationship between man and machine were the topics up for discussion at the European Innovation Partnership event. Prior to the event, graphic recorder Sebastian Lörscher decided to make the dialogue between human and machine the central theme of the recording.

Because the recording was planned in advance, he had time to consider how to communicate this concept in a clear way and decided ultimately on geometric forms in which the machine speaks in circles and the person in squares. In the end, they find a way to communicate in triangles. As an element, the triangle reappears in the final image as well as in the pyramid where the man on top reaches for the star.

The theme and the layout, which required client approval before moving forward, were the complete opposite of a typical spontaneous recording. This resulted in Lörscher redrawing the preplanned image live during the event. Although a fan of the improvisational nature of traditional graphic recording and the happy accidents that can lead to exciting new solutions, the pre-event development process and final piece were visually interesting and effectively communicated the event's message.

—

WHAT'S NEXT, EIP?/SMART CITIES
fig. 1

Client: European Innovation Partnership
Produced in: Germany, 2015
Technique: Analog
Format: Keynote and conference
Dimensions: 1.5 x 2 m
Time: 1 hour

fig. 1

THE VALUE WEB

—

Sita Magnuson
Alicia Bramlett

—

thevalueweb.org

—

Detail zoom

This large-scale knowledge wall weaves key concepts from plenary sessions and group breakouts together with the core concept of the symposium: turning what we know into what we do.

Looking for big, bold graphics that could anchor the 2.4 × 8.5 meters wall, graphic recorders Sita Magnuson and Alicia Bramlett knew they wanted to play with visuals relating to children and early childhood development. They also knew that a well-thought-out process for integrating content from the sessions into the larger knowledge wall was key to a successful piece. Once they had a system in place, it would be easy to combine.

Materials became an important part of the process as well. Black paint covered the background, while white and colored acrylic paint markers drew attention to the core concepts by differentiating what we know versus what we do. Additionally, strong visuals connected the different sections to one another, guiding the viewer's eye through the image.

—

ACCELERATING INNOVATION:
TELLING THE BRAIN STORY TO
INSPIRE ACTION
fig. 1

Client: Palix Foundation
Produced in: Edmonton, Canada, 2013
Technique: Analog
Format: Keynotes and workshops
Dimensions: 2.4 × 8.5 m
Time: 6 days

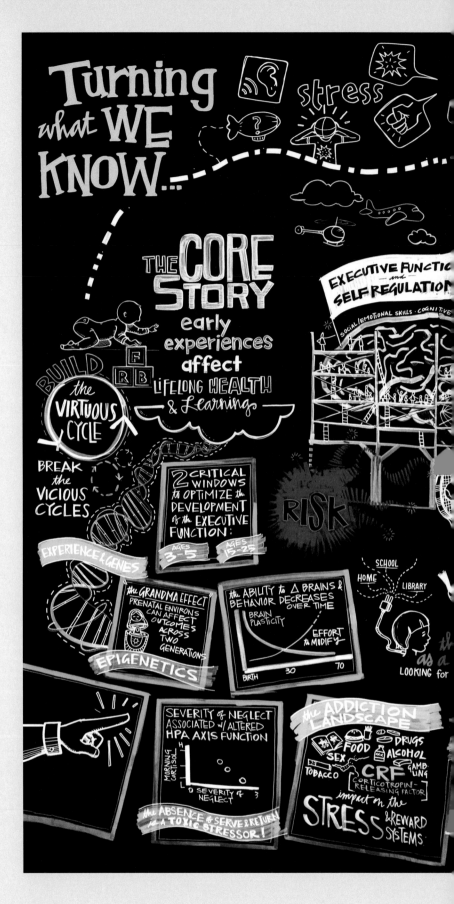

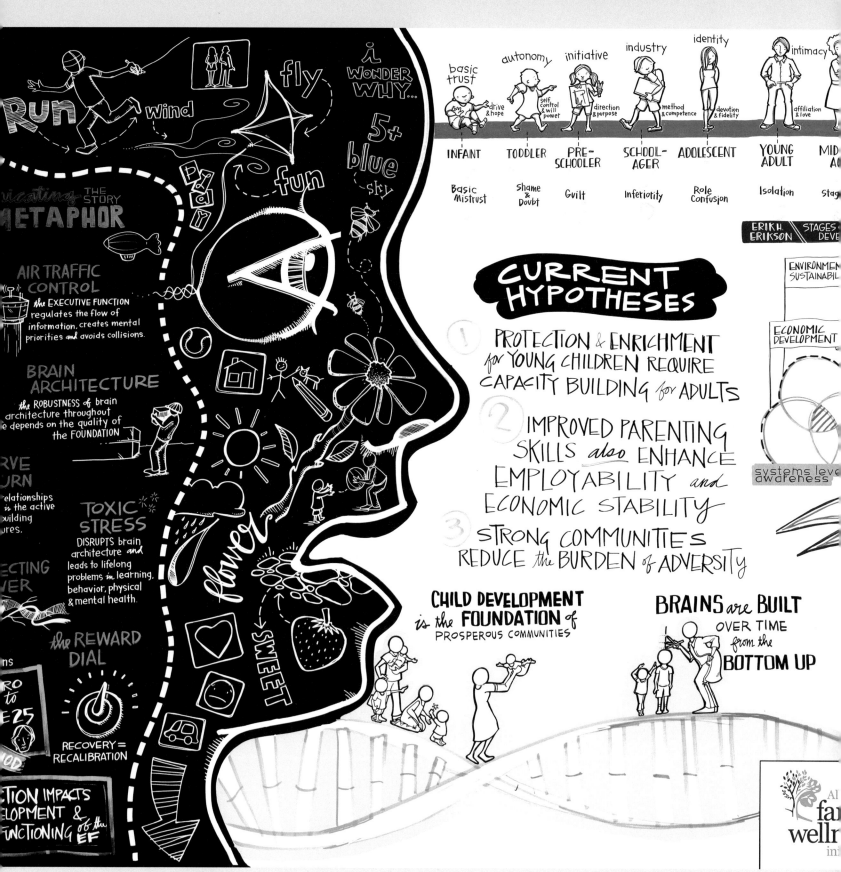

fig. 1

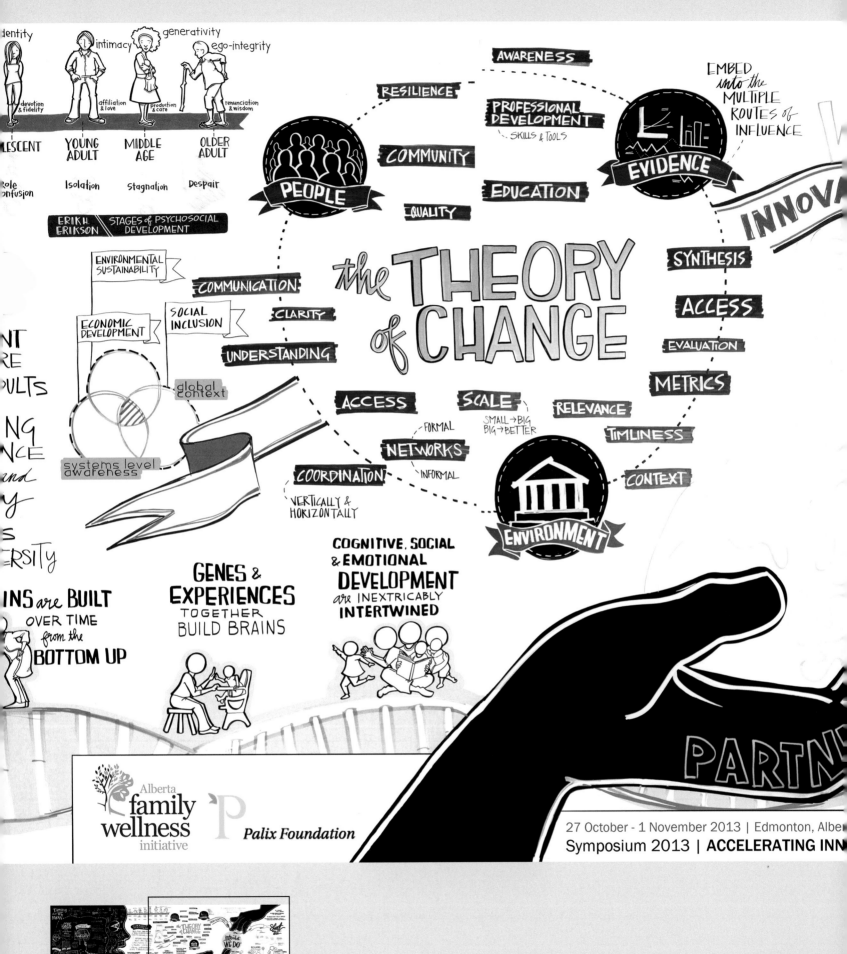

the **THEORY** of **CHANGE**

PEOPLE
- RESILIENCE
- PROFESSIONAL DEVELOPMENT — SKILLS & TOOLS
- COMMUNITY
- EDUCATION
- QUALITY
- AWARENESS

EVIDENCE
- EMBED *into the* MULTIPLE ROUTES *of* INFLUENCE
- SYNTHESIS
- ACCESS
- EVALUATION
- METRICS
- RELEVANCE
- TIMLINESS
- CONTEXT

INNOVA

ENVIRONMENT
- ACCESS
- SCALE — SMALL→BIG, BIG→BETTER
- NETWORKS — FORMAL / INFORMAL
- COORDINATION — VERTICALLY & HORIZONTALLY

- COMMUNICATION
- CLARITY
- UNDERSTANDING
- SOCIAL INCLUSION
- global context
- systems level awareness

ENVIRONMENTAL SUSTAINABILITY

ECONOMIC DEVELOPMENT

identity
intimacy
generativity
ego-integrity

devotion & fidelity
affiliation & love
production & care
renunciation & wisdom

ESCENT / YOUNG ADULT / MIDDLE AGE / OLDER ADULT

role onfusion / Isolation / Stagnation / Despair

ERIK H. ERIKSON — STAGES *of* PSYCHOSOCIAL DEVELOPMENT

NT RE DULTS NG NCE and y S RSITY

INS *are* BUILT OVER TIME *from the* BOTTOM UP

GENES & EXPERIENCES TOGETHER BUILD BRAINS

COGNITIVE, SOCIAL & EMOTIONAL DEVELOPMENT *are* INEXTRICABLY INTERTWINED

PARTN

Alberta family wellness initiative

P Palix Foundation

27 October - 1 November 2013 | Edmonton, Albe
Symposium 2013 | **ACCELERATING INN**

Detail zoom

Telling the Brain Story to Inspire Action

CREATIVE **HUB** DIRECTORY   CENTRAL VOICE

RESOURCE BANK APP

PARTNER

INVEST PATRONS GRANTS

CHAMBER OF C·R·E·A·T·I·V·E COMMERCES

ELECTRONIC NETWORKING   COLORADO CREATES

YOUTH Art in Schools

TAKE RISK

PARTNERSHIPS

FUTURE GENERAT ALL AGES

MENTORSHIPS INTERNSHIPS CLEARINGHOUSE

VOLUNTEERS AMBASSADORS

ART IS Essential

INTERTWINING throughout the COMMUNITY

MEASURE

Economic Impact

Art in ALTERNATIVE Spaces

graffiti flash mob

COLORADO CREATIVE INDUSTRIES SUMMIT

APRIL 12 & 13, 2012

Cultivating   Comr

fig. 1

HEATHER MARTINEZ

—

heathermartinez.com

—

In an effort to promote and enrich the arts in its home state, the Colorado Council for the Arts hosted a Creative Industries Summit in the city of Boulder. Graphic recorder Heather Martinez joined the team not only to visualize and record the event, but also to help design a program that could achieve the summit's desired goals and to provide engaging content for the final graphic recording.

After considering the large number of participants, Martinez decided to create a facilitation plan that included an illustrated guide for transitioning the plenary session into seven breakout groups. Each group had the opportunity to get to know one another, brainstorm ideas, and present them to the larger group using templates drawn ahead of time by Martinez. The templates served not only as a structure for filtering and recording the 400+ ideas generated in the breakout groups, but also as a way of creating consistency for the final piece. After a round of voting, the top ten ideas were captured and participants encouraged to volunteer to help make the ideas a reality.

The final piece was shared with the client, who paired Martinez's graphic recording with a video from the conference.

—

COLORADO CREATIVE INDUSTRIES SUMMIT
fig. 1

Client: Colorado Council for the Arts
Produced in: Boulder, CO, USA
Technique: Analog
Format: Workshop
Dimensions: 1.2 × 2.4 m
Time: 45 minutes

MEDIUM CREATIVE FACILITATION

—

Jorge Merchán

—

cfmedium.com

—

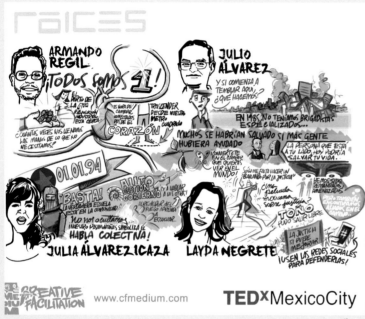

fig. 1

The independently organized TEDx conferences were conceived as local experiences that can maximize the TED mission of sharing ideas. In 2016, TEDxMexico City was designed to encourage a new creative, powerful, critical, and daring generation to use disruptive thoughts and ideas to build a more dynamic city. Graphic recorder Jorge Enrique Merchán Vidal created graphic digital summaries of the TEDx sessions. His choice to work digitally had a number of advantages for both the audience and himself; the audience could easily watch the progress of the recording on a screen, while Photoshop gave Vidal access to a large range of tools as well as the option to quickly erase marks. Although useful, Photoshop is a resource that if not used wisely, can tempt the recorder to focus more on design rather than extracting the main ideas from the content. One of the basic components of Vidal's work is the notion of life and motion; his background in cartooning enables him to animate his stories with characters. For TEDx, he drew a caricature of each speaker ahead of time. The caricatures then

became a starting point for the graphic metaphors created from each presentation. It is also always important to consider any comment that evoked a reaction from the audience because they are the anchors for a memorable message; using elements from the speech for each character, he created volume with multiple layers and textures, and emphasized key messages with larger fonts.

—

TEDX FOR MEXICO CITY
fig. 1–2

Client: TEDxMéxico City
Produced in: Mexico City, Mexico, 2016
Technique: Digital
Format: Keynote
Dimensions: 3.65 × 3 m
Time: 45 minutes each

—

INC MONTERREY
fig. 3–6

Client: Instituto Tecnológico de Monterrey – Mexico
Produced in: Mexico City, Mexico, 2015
Technique: Analog
Format: Conference
Dimensions: 12.2 × 18.3 m
Time: 7 hours

RDILLO

ABLE, 1. ENCUENTRA TU MANERA

IBLE 2. ANALIZA, ¿POR QUÉ QUIERES SEGUIR ADELANTE

OY EL OR MPLO!

E! 3. PIENSA DIFERENTE DESARROLLA TUS CAPACIDADES

LETICIA GASCA

→ ACEPTARLO
→ COMPARTIRLO
→ ESTUDIARLO

EL FRACASO ES MÁS COMÚN QUE EL ÉXITO

MI NEGOCIO ES DE MUJERES, TENGO MENOS POSIBILIDAD DE FRACASAR

LAS HISTORIAS DE ÉXITO SON INCOMPLETAS

VULNERABLE = FELIZ

COMPARTE TU HISTORIA

NDA

OS EL NDO PARA AR NUESTRO

KM DE CUEVAS

N TESORO ARQUEOLÓGICO

OMO LAS CAVERNAS, ESTAMOS CONECTADOS A LOS ECOSISTEMAS

MARIANA VALDEZ

علیکم السلام
CREER EN 1 SÓLO DIOS Y SUS PROFETAS

LAS MUJERES NOS CUBRIMOS PORQUE SOMOS LA BASE, SERVIMOS A DIOS, NUESTRA BELLEZA ESTÁ RESERVADA PARA NUESTRAS FAMILIAS

APAGUEN LA TELE

¡ENCUENTREN SU VERDAD!

ALVAR SAENZ OTERO

ROMPIENDO FRONTERAS, PENSANDO MÁS ALLÁ DE LA TIERRA

OS HISPANOAMERICANAS?

PLACES TUS SUEÑOS POR

SÁCALOS DE TU MALETA, NO CARGUES CON LOS MIEDOS DE LOS OTROS, NO ERES PERFECTA

ENCIA N IENTO

IZA NIO

HOMBRES... JUEGUEN EN EQUIPO

SIENDO NIÑO ME DI CUENTA DE EL ESPACIO YA N DERA LA ÚLTIMA FRONTERA

NUESTRA ATMÓSFERA ES MUY DÉBIL

¡RÉTENSE!

YO NAVEGO A BASE DE VISIÓN, IGNORO LO QUE NO VEO... (COMO LA BASURA ESPACIAL...)

TRABAJAMOS EN EL ENSAMBLAJE AUTOMÁTICO DE ESTACIONES ESPACIALES PARA PODER IR A MARTE!

MUCHOS SATÉLITES PEQUEÑOS EN ÓRBITA NOS AYUDARÁN A MONITOREAR LA TIERRA PARA PROTEGERLA...

TEDxMexicoCity

fig. 2

fig. 3

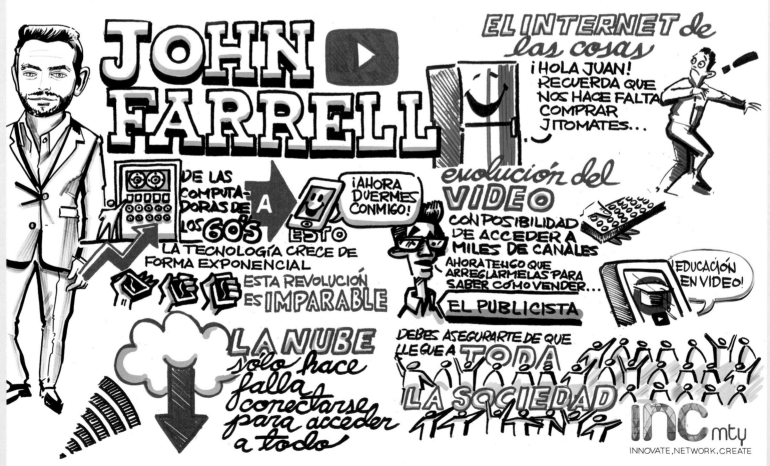

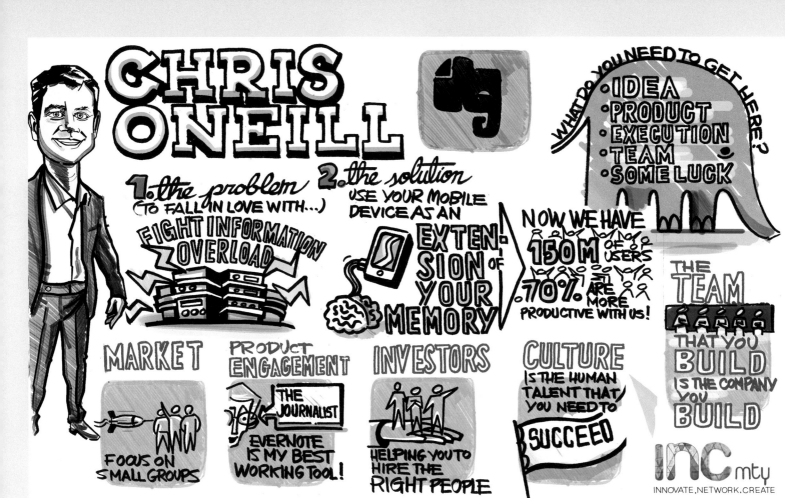

fig. 5

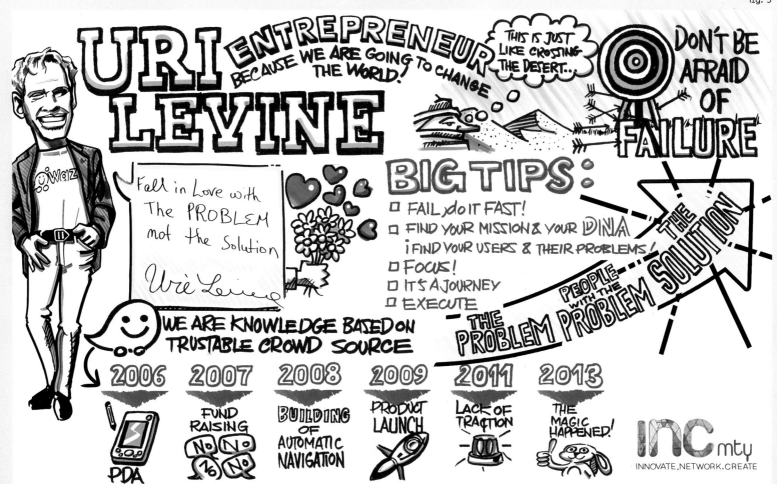

MEDIUM CREATIVE FACILITATION

fig. 6

TAK-TIK

—

Tikka Hun

—

tak-tik.com

–

The Kantar space illustration created by Tak-Tik at the 2015 APAC Conference translated insights from the event onto a large chalkboard wall that allowed participants to interact during the five-day event. Run by GroupM, the world's largest media investment company, the event gathered together a whopping 800 participants from the advertising and media world. For the participants, the graphic recording transformed complex and possibly boring data into something tangible and interesting. For Tak-Tik's Tikka Hun, who became a graphic recorder after ten years of working as an art director, it was a logical transition because both jobs communicate concepts visually. Tak-Tik's drawing style also comes from the world of commercial drawing with its emphasis on clear marks, fast working methods, and an understanding that the drawing is only a tool instead of the end result. For Tak-Tik, a successful recording begins with a preliminary design that captures the objective of the event using the corporate logo or colors, or finding an image that represents the intended message. The challenge then becomes creating the work as fast as the spoken word. Ultimately, a successful graphic recording includes rich content that also reflects the flow and pattern of the conversation, which is impossible to know ahead of time.

—

KANTAR SPACE ILLUSTRATION
fig. 1–4

Client: Kantar
Produced in: Bali, Indonesia, 2015
Technique: Analog
Format: Conference
Dimensions: 10 × 3 m
Time: 4 days

fig. 1

fig. 2

fig. 3

fig. 4

SKETCH POST

—

sketchpost.com

—

When Zoetis hosted a forum for its most valued customers, they invited creativity and innovation expert Scott Anthony as the speaker. Wanting to encourage new ways of thinking, Anthony chose Sketch Post to help inspire participants to rethink the creative process in their own businesses.

Keeping in mind that the majority of the audience came from South East Asian countries, the team made an effort to keep the language simple while staying true to Scott's content by emphasizing pictures and icons to elaborate on main points. Because Zoetis is an animal health company, animal characters were a natural iconic image to represent ideas about innovation, while human characters represented the audience and their role in the innovation process.

Stylistically, Sketch Post keeps color to a minimum and tends instead towards bold, dynamic lines. Starting with black outlines and colorful highlights that guide the viewer's eye, they also favor bold, black shapes that add visual weight to their work. In this case, they chose red as the hero color because it worked well with Zoetis's corporate orange, producing a fiery combination that gave the design a strong sense of movement.

—

**ASEAN TOP CUSTOMER FORUM 2015
BY ZOETIS**
fig. 1–3

Client: Zoetis Thailand
Produced in: Bangkok, Thailand, 2015
Technique: Analog
Format: Keynote and workshop
Dimensions: 1.2 x 2.4 m each
Time: 8 hours

—

LEAN IN SUMMIT MALAYSIA 2015
fig. 4–5

Client: Lean in Malaysia
Produced in: Kuala Lumpur, Malaysia, 2015
Technique: Analog
Format: Keynote
Dimensions: 0.9 x 1.8 m each
Time: 8 hours

fig. 2

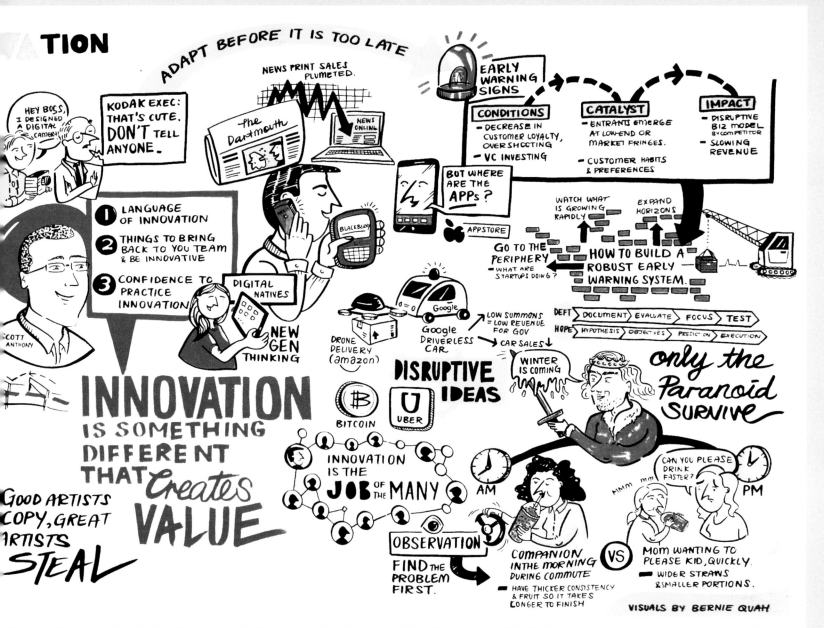

fig. 1

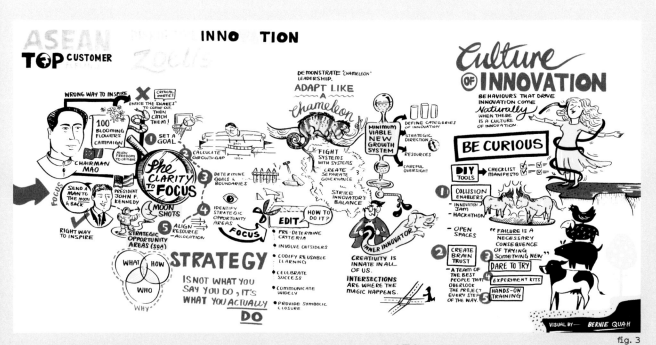

fig. 3

fig. 4

SKETCH POST

fig. 5

GRAPHIC RECORDING NETWORK BERLIN

—

Gabriele Schlipf
Michael Schrenk

—

momik.de
live-illustration.de

—

When graphic recorders work as a team, an added layer of planning is needed to make the event a success. When Gabriele Schlipf and Michael Schrenk prepared for BASF's 150th anniversary celebration in Ludwigshafen, Germany, they needed not only to plan graphic decisions, but also how to best work together within the specific parameters of the event. As members of the Graphic Recording Network Berlin, the two had previous experience working simultaneously on individual pieces—but this time it was clear that they would need to interweave their styles onto the same canvas.

After capturing all of the plenary sessions over the course of two days, they connected the sessions, transitions, and the order of the agenda items with square elements inspired by the BASF logo. For the six parallel workshops on renewable energy forms, they arranged the information in such a way that their styles alternated, allowing them to work comfortably without blocking each other. After two days it was clearly a successful approach; the organic flow of the plenary piece transported the energy of the event while the more structured layouts reflected the hard work and the inspiring ideas of the workshop sessions.

—

CREATOR SPACE™ TOUR LUDWIGSHAFEN
fig. 1–2

Client: BASF AG
Produced in: Ludwigshafen, Germany, 2015
Technique: Analog
Format: Workshops and conferences
Dimensions: 1.5 × 3.2 m each
Time: 2 days

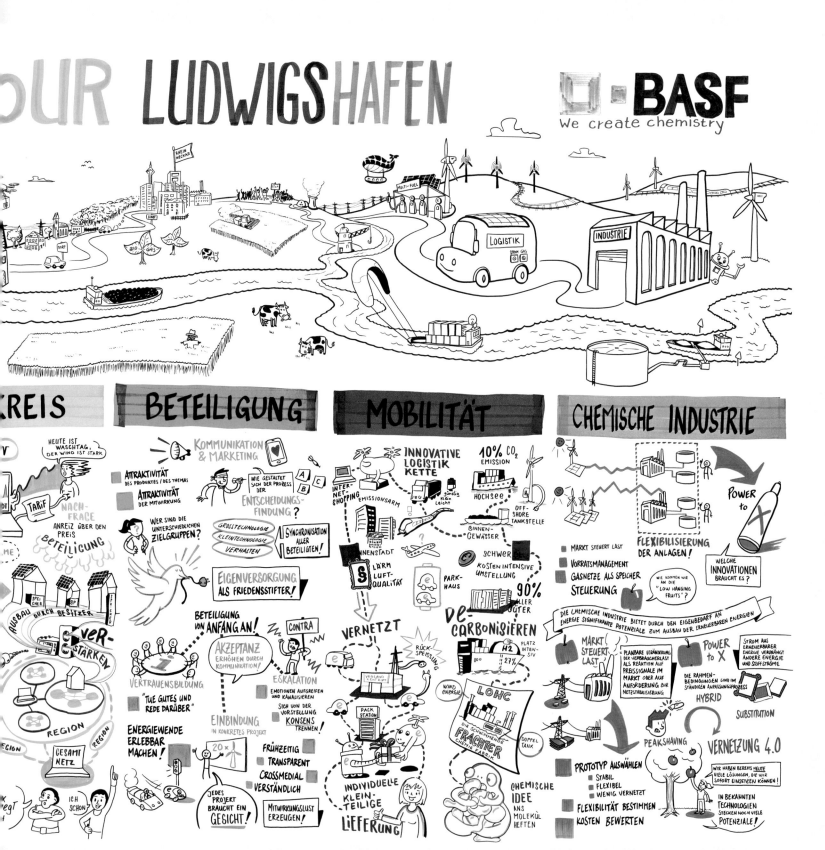

fig. 1

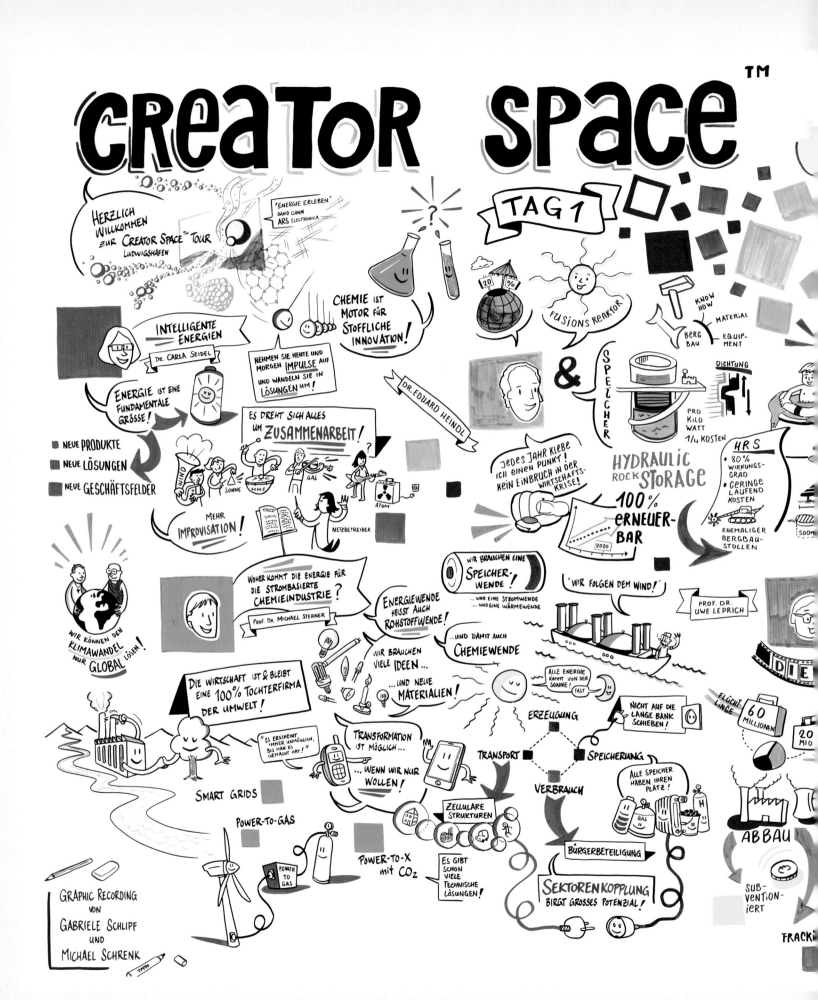

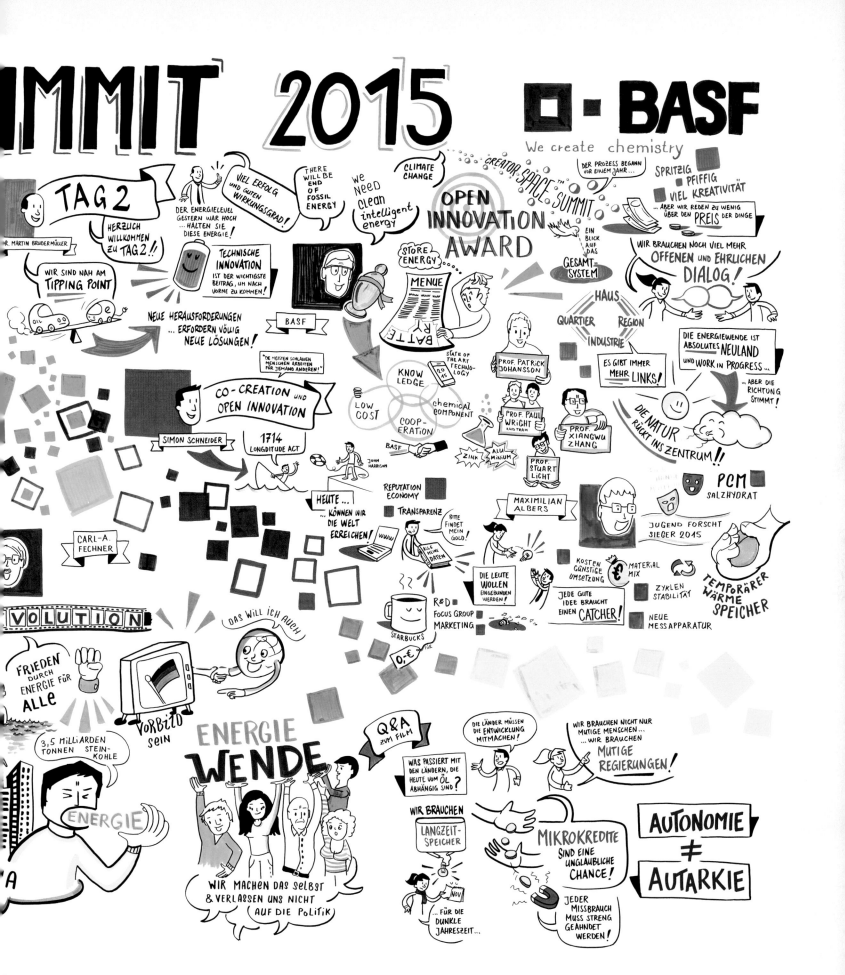

MOMIK*

—

Gabriele Schlipf

—

momik.de

—

fig. 1

Gabriele Schlipf identifies not just as a graphic recorder but as a translator, an attitude particularly well-suited for her work at Berlin's Staatliche Museen during its symposium on plaster casting. The symposium, which required her to capture scientific lectures and discussions in both German and English, is an example of the intense concentration and flexibility required of a graphic recorder.

With multiple lectures, keynotes, and discussions packed into just two days, she managed to create 12 final panels using a well-thought-out visual strategy. Because the speakers were talking about visible art, the first step was to ensure ahead of time that the sculptures were sketched accurately. Starting with the bust of Nefertiti—a focal point of the symposium—she drew multiple versions of its silhouette for use throughout the recording. In order to mirror the form of plaster casts, she divided a three-dimensional

structure for the panels by first cutting out the silhouette of Nefertiti and then using the rest of the foam board as a negative form.

Knowing she wanted the final work to look like art rather than an Excel spreadsheet, she color-coded the lectures, using yellow and red for the past and green and blue for the present and future. The introduction and the final discussion combine both colors.

—

CASTING. A WAY TO EMBRACE THE DIGITAL AGE IN ANALOGUE FASHION? A SYMPOSIUM ON THE GIPSFORMEREI OF THE STAATLICHE MUSEEN ZU BERLIN, 2015
fig. 1–3

Client: Staatliche Museen zu Berlin, Stiftung Preußischer Kulturbesitz
Produced in: Berlin, Germany, 2015
Technique: Analog
Format: Keynotes and conferences
Dimensions: 1 x 0.7 m each
Time: 2 days

179

fig. 2

fig. 3

PATALETA
—
Zulma Patarroyo
—
pataleta.net
—

The Forum for East Asia and Latin America Cooperation helps member countries share experience and knowledge to enhance socio-economic development. The first thing

graphic recorder Zulma Patarroyo drew when arriving at the event was a welcome chart that included a map of its members that stood as a reminder of the multicultural spirit of cooperation running through the event. Although English was a second language for most of the participants, talks were given in English to non-native speakers, while comments and questions were made in Spanish. In this context, the graphic recording helped facilitate clear dialogue, exploration, and understanding. Formal elements such as typography and graphic style worked together with less formal aspects to invite participants to explore and create something new together.

As a networking event where people also represented their organizations, logos were an important graphic tool for helping audience

members easily associate speakers with the content of their presentations. Talks were grouped according to topic on a single chart with a color code separating each presentation. In this way the reader could see different perspectives on one topic while still being able to distinguish the presentations from each other.

—

FINANCING INNOVATION AND DYNAMIC ENTREPRENEURSHIP FORUM
fig. 1–2

Client: FEALAC – Forum for East Asia and Latin America Cooperation
Produced in: Bogotá, Colombia, 2015
Technique: Analog
Format: Keynote
Dimensions: 3 x 1 m
Time: 10 hours

fig. 1

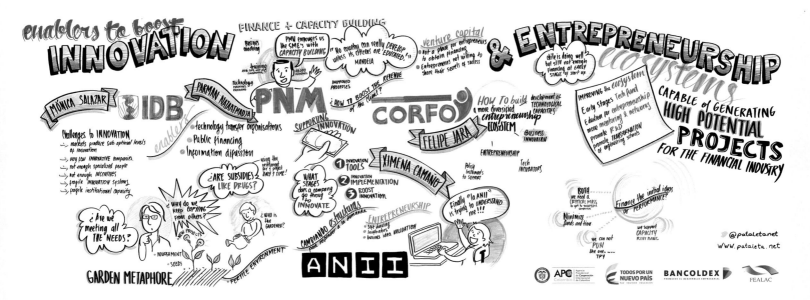

fig. 2

HOLGER NILS POHL

—

holgernilspohl.de

—

Once a week, Holger Nils Pohl and his team create a graphic recording for the Innovation Ecosystem podcast. The ongoing project, conceived with the podcast's creator, initially presented a number of challenges for Pohl, including the need to find a work system that allowed his team to produce quality visuals every week of the year. After weeks of consideration, they decided to produce the recordings with an iPad and the WorkVisual app, which immediately provides a shareable digital image as well as video of the drawing process. Choosing the iPad as a drawing tool also opened up the process to possibilities beyond analog drawing: now the graphic recorder can quickly fill large areas with color or get second (or third) chances at refining rogue lines.

Due to the podcast production process, Pohl and team must work from transcripts rather than audio files. A traditional graphic recording session allows the recorder to simultaneously listen and make visual decisions about the interpretation. Working from interview transcripts, on the other hand, requires the graphic recorder to work in a more disjointed way as they read, process, and then draw. Because the recorder can't do these tasks at the same time, it is a special skill to maintain an overarching picture of the topic rather than getting enmeshed in the details.

—

INNOVATION ECOSYSTEM
fig. 1

Client: Innovation Ecosystem Podcast
Produced in: Cologne, Germany, 2016
Technique: digital, iPad, WorkVisual App
Format: Interviews
Dimensions: 4:3 Ratio, iPadPro Resolution Exporter to DINA4 and DINA6 and 1080p HD video
Time: 6 hours each week

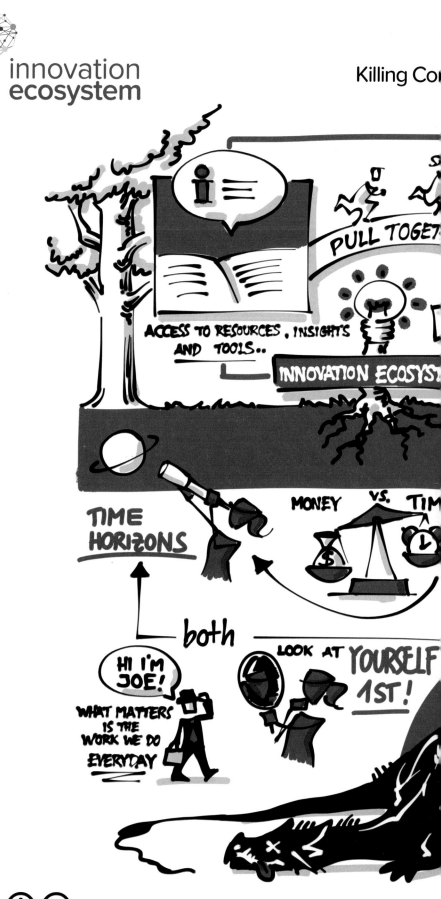

Visuals created by WorkVisual Institute

fig. 1

SCRIBERIA

—

scriberia.co.uk

—

In 2012, filmmaker David Bond launched a campaign called Project Wild Thing that encouraged parents and children to spend more time outdoors connecting with nature. Scriberia were invited to record the project's workshops that reimagined nature and inspired children to take care of it. Starting with common barriers that prevent kids from engaging with the outdoors, Scriberia used markers on paper to bring the conversation to life and to make it easily shared with a wider audience. The style of the recording, which hits just the right balance between cartoon, graphic design, storytelling, and content mapping, tells the story of the day on two levels. First, it breaks up the content into separate, easy-to-read issues and questions. Second, it encroaches on the drawing space in the same way building developments and indoor lifestyles have encroached on nature. Their bold, simple use of color and line are important. There's no shading or tone—just a strong graphic approach. Everything Scriberia draws—including the typography—works to support and reinforce the overall story they are trying to tell.

—

PROJECT WILD THING
fig. 1

Client: Good for Nothing
Produced in: London, United Kingdom, 2012
Technique: Analog
Format: Workshop
Dimensions: 4.5 x 1.5 m
Time: 4 hours

—

THINK CREATE DO
fig. 2–3

Client: Creative Quarter, Nottingham
Produced in: Nottingham, United Kingdom, 2015
Technique: Analog
Format: Keynotes
Dimensions: 0.3 x 0.4 m each
Time: 1.5 hours

—

TOYOTA GENEVA
fig. 4

Client: Toyota Europe
Produced in: Geneva, Switzerland, 2015
Technique: Analog
Format: Tradeshow
Dimensions: 1.5 x 4 m
Time: 5 hours

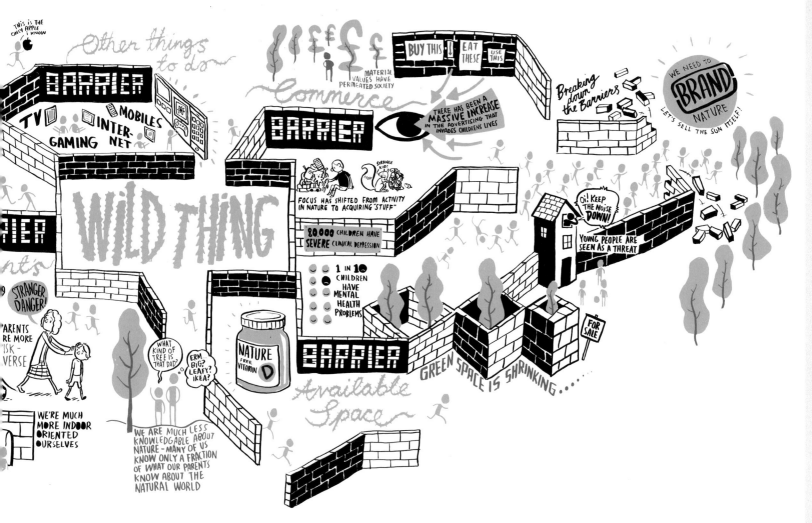

fig. 1

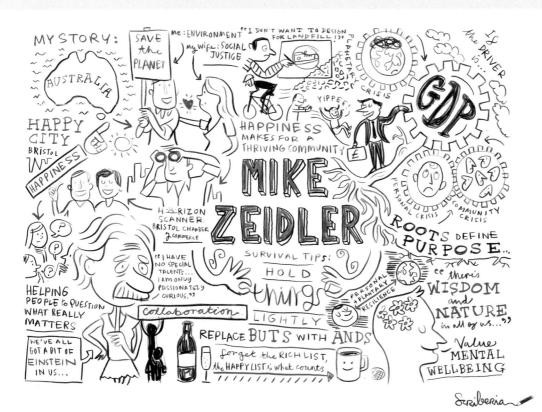

fig. 2

fig. 3

fig. 4

Index

GRAPHIC RECORDING

—

Live Illustrations
for Meetings, Conferences
and Workshops

—

This book was conceived, edited, and designed by Gestalten.

Edited by Robert Klanten, Anna Lena Schiller, and Sven Ehmann

Chapter 1–3: Background and how-to by Anna Lena Schiller
Chapter 4: Project texts by Rebecca Silus

Texts edited by Kevin Brochet-Nguyen and Noelia Hobeika
Editorial Management by Sina Kernstock
Proofreading by Transparent Language Solutions

Creative Direction of Design by Ludwig Wendt
Layout by Léon Giogoli
Cover design by Ludwig Wendt
Typefaces: Hermes by Gavillet & Rust; Minion Pro by Robert Slimbach
Cover image by Jongens van de Tekeningen
Back cover images by Sita Magnuson and Alicia Bramlett (top), Joel Cooper
(middle), Stephanie von Becker (bottom left), Gabriele Schlipf (bottom right)

Printed by Nino Druck GmbH, Neustadt/Weinstr.
Made in Germany

Published by Gestalten, Berlin 2016
ISBN 978-3-89955-656-8

German Edition, ISBN 978-3-89955-692-6

—

© Die Gestalten Verlag GmbH & Co. KG, Berlin 2016

Bibliographic information published by the Deutsche Nationalbibliothek.
The Deutsche Nationalbibliothek lists this publication in the Deutsche Nationalbibliografie; detailed bibliographic data are available online at http://dnb.d-nb.de.

None of the content in this book was published in exchange for payment by commercial parties or designers; Gestalten selected all included work based solely on its artistic merit.

This book was printed on paper certified according to the standard of FSC®.